77 TALKS FOR 21ST CENTURY KIDS

77 TALKS
FOR
21st CENTURY KIDS

CHRIS CHESTERTON

MONARCH

Crowborough

British Library Cataloguing Data
A catalogue record for this book is available
from the British Library.

ISBN 1 85424 388 8

Text design and layout by Alex Marsden

Designed and produced by Bookprint Creative Services
P.O. Box 827, BN21 3YJ, England for
MONARCH PUBLICATIONS
Broadway House, The Broadway
Crowborough, East Sussex, TN6 1HQ.
Printed in Great Britain.

CONTENTS

INTRODUCTION

"Look at this belt," says Jeremiah, holding the rotting strip under the noses of his hearers. "The man who wore this would end up with his trousers round his ankles!"

"Look at these beautiful wild flowers under your feet," says Jesus. "Look at that flock of birds feeding over there ..."

CRASH! goes the mud brick wall of Ezekiel's house as he kicks his way through it. It is a wordless parable that brings a crowd running to peer through the dust.

That's how God's word goes out. That's how the great communicators of the Bible unblocked ears to hear the message.

But surely the eyes of today's kids are too dazzled by flickering screens to see? Surely their ears are too blasted by techno-beat to hear? Surely we can't compete with marketing men, budgets of billions, cutting-edge electronics?

WRONG!

This generation of kids is force-fed on entertainment and information coming through a glass brightly. It is a diet high in sugar and spice but low in real nutrition. These children are starving for meaningful human contact. Just being there in the flesh carries a premium, being there with a message to share and a love that burns to break the communication barrier.

What was the greatest act of communication of all time? – the Word made flesh. "**We saw it,**" says John, getting excited. "**We heard it. We touched it.**" Interactive? Absolutely!

These 77 messages for kids are modelled on the examples of Jesus and the prophets. They take the stuff of the world at the turn of the millennium and use it as a lens to focus truth from beyond time. They are interactive in a way the touch-pad and keyboard can never be.

Adapt them to your own circumstances, expand them, or use them as a spur to developing your own ideas. Tell them with humour and humility. Communicate with confidence in the Creator, and with an awed respect for the sacred right of each precious child both to hear and to choose freely.

"We write this to you so that you can be full of joy with us," John continues in his First Letter. That is my motivation for writing these 'messages with a meaning'. I hope you will share it as motivation for taking them out to a spiritually hungry generation.

Chris Chesterton

Nottingham, May 1997

Chris Chesterton is Director of CENS (Christian Education in Nottingham Schools) and has sixteen years experience working in schools and churches with children and young people. He is married to Sheila and they have three grown-up children. As well as the kind of material in this book, he uses drama and ventriloquism to hold the attention of his young audiences. He is co-author of *A Really Great Assembly* (Scripture Union, 1992) and *52 Ideas For Junior Classroom Assemblies* (Monarch, 1995).

These talks are revised versions of ones which first appeared in ASSEMBLY LINE, a termly collection of material for people who lead school acts of worship. It is published by CENS.

For more information write to CENS, 94 Burlington Road, Sherwood, Nottingham NG5 2GS or see the website:
http://www.innotts.co.uk/~cens/

With thanks for their invaluable contributions to:
Nigel Lee, David Smith, Malcolm Rogers, Pat Gutteridge, Catherine Aldridge, Allan Tibble and Ian Blake for their ideas, contributions and stories; James Walton for the illustrations; and Alex Marsden for the design and layout.

GOD, YOU & ME

GOD IS ETERNAL

✦ THEME
Thinking about the nature of God has always been part of human life.

✦ YOU WILL NEED
- a board or O.H.P. to write on
- examples of some hieroglyphics or Chinese characters

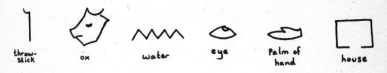

throw-stick   ox   water   eye   Palm of hand   house

✦ PRESENTATION
Write silently as children watch:

'You shall give Ababu eight portions of ... '

Those words were written on the wall of an Egyptian turquoise mine in the Sinai Desert 4500 years ago. We do not know who Ababu was, or what he was to be given eight portions of. The end of the sentence has been lost with time. Presumably it wasn't a take-away pizza!
(Children might like to make some guesses.)

But the words are very important, not for *what* they say but for *how they were written*. The words carved on the walls of this Egyptian mine are the earliest in the world to be written in an alphabet of just a few letters. Before that, all writing was in hieroglyphics – a different picture or symbol for each word (**show examples**). Just imagine what it would be like in school if instead of making words out of just twenty-six letters you had to know a different picture-character for

5

every word! It would be like writing in Chinese. The alphabet is one of the great human inventions of all time.

A TIMELESS MESSAGE

There is another sentence carved on the wall of this mine. This is what it says (write silently):

'God is eternal.'

God is eternal. He never changes. He is beyond time. He existed before the Universe was created and will continue after it has ended.

Written words can be used for simple practical messages like, 'Please remember to lock the door when you go out' or, 'Give Abubu eight portions of sweet and sour camel.' They can also be used for messages that are for all time and for all people. Not far away from this mine is Mount Sinai, where God gave Moses the Ten Commandments. But a thousand years before that a humble miner knew and wrote a great truth: 'God is eternal.'

✦ A PRAYER

Here is a prayer from a letter in the Bible written 2500 years after that miner lived:

> **Now to the King, eternal, immortal, invisible, the only God, be honour and glory for ever and ever. Amen.**
>
> *1 Timothy 1:17, New International Version*

Adapted from an article by Jamie Buckingham in GOOD NEWS Newsletter.

THUNDER FROM HEAVEN

✦ THEME
For the morning after the thunder-storm the night before, we link some factual information with one of David's biblical songs of praise.

✦ YOU WILL NEED
- the means of creating 'virtual' thunder and lightning. For lightning, flash some lights or use a camera flash. For thunder, hold a large sheet of cardboard by the edge and shake it, or drum on the side of a box.
- a Bible: *2 Samuel 22:5-20*. Have a group or individual prepare to read this dramatically. Treat it as a piece of theatre, to be read with as much power and drama as possible.

✦ PRESENTATION
Refer to any recent thunderstorm, or to an experience you had in the past. Thunder and lightning frighten some people and excite others. Whichever kind of way you react, you can hardly ignore lightning if it strikes close to you. Lightning is a giant spark leaping between a cloud and the earth. The temperature generated by that spark reaches around 30,000°. This causes the air to expand at supersonic speed. It is this explosion of hot air along the lightning's path that we hear as thunder.

Most people know that you can tell roughly how far away the lightning is by counting the seconds between seeing the flash and hearing the thunder. Does anyone know why? ... It is because light travels so fast we see the lightning virtually at once, but sound travels much slower, around one-third of a kilometre per second. That gives us the answer to how far away the storm is: one-third of a kilometre for each second we count, or three seconds for each kilometre.

Try that out. Teach the children to count roughly seconds using the word 'seconds' in between each number: **'one second, two seconds, three seconds'**, etc.. The stopwatch function on a wristwatch is useful. Now present your 'virtual thunderstorm'. Get the children to count between the 'lightning' and the 'thunder' and then tell you how far away the 'storm' is.

In the past, people sometimes thought of thunderstorms as the work of the gods. The Norse god Thor was the god of thunder. But even when we know the scientific explanations, the awesome power of a thunderstorm can still make us realise how small we are. The power of natural phenomena like this has often reminded people of the power of God. If you know that God is loving, then that power can be reassuring rather than frightening.

This was true for David, the same David who killed Goliath and later had to run and hide from the anger of King Saul. He once wrote a song about a time when everything seemed so bad that he felt like giving up. Then a great thunderstorm reminded him of the power of God, the God he knew cared for him and protected him. Now listen to part of that song.

Present the reading of *2 Samuel 22:5-20.*

KANGAROOS AND MANNA

✦ THEME
Examples of God providing in desperate situations.

✦ PRESENTATION
Tell children you have a game for them to play on teachers, parents, or other unsuspecting adults: when asked a question to which they don't know the answer, they reply, 'Kangaroo'.

Practise with a few suitable questions, eg Who was number one in the charts on January 1st 1983? ...

What are the names of the Queen's corgis? ...

How high is the tallest mountain in Africa? ...

When the teacher or parent becomes exasperated with this silly behaviour, they can explain that they are simply practicing the Australian Aborigine language. Captain James Cook and his expedition were the first Europeans to set foot in Australia. They made contact with the Aborigines and began to learn a few words of the Aboriginal language. When Cook asked what the funny jumping animals were, the Aborigines replied, 'I don't know'. In their language that is pronounced 'kangaroo'. So to this day there are millions of 'I don't knows' hopping about Australia!

BREAKFASTING ON WOTSIT
Another strange word like that comes from the story of the Israelite people when they were in the desert after escaping from slavery in Egypt. Food was short and the Israelites began to complain that they would die of hunger. Their leader, Moses, prayed to God, and in the morning the ground was covered all over with white flakes, like frost. The people were all saying, 'What is it? What is it?'

Finally someone dared taste it – it was like honey-flavoured wafers. If you had been an Israelite child your parents would probably have given you a jar and told you to go and collect some of that ... er ... some of that 'wotsit'. The Israelite word for 'wotsit' was *manna*. So the Israelites were saved from starvation by eating honey-flavoured manna or 'wotsit'.

You might still hear that word today. On the A60 outside Nottingham, for example, is a farm called Manna Farm – that is m-a-n-n-a not m-a-n-o-r. It is a place where drug-addicts can go and learn how to live without drugs. Manna

Farm was set up by Christians, some of whom had problems with drugs themselves in the past. They called it Manna Farm because, just as the Israelites believed God sent the manna to rescue them when they were in a desperate situation, the farm helps rescue people today who are desperate.

A possible final word: By the way, don't overdo it with the kangaroo game – you might just find an exasperated parent sends you to bed early with a kick up the ... er ... *manna*!

✦ SOMETHING TO THINK ABOUT
David's experience when he was in a desperate situation:

> I asked the Lord for help and he
> answered me. He saved me from all
> that I feared. Those who go to him for help
> are happy. They are never disgraced.
>
> *Psalm 34:4-5*

WITH OUR OWN EYES

This little demonstration of balance is hard to believe, but very easy to do. Try it and amaze yourself – and the children!

✦ THEME
Some things are hard to believe until you see them with your own eyes.

✦ YOU WILL NEED
- an ordinary 30cm ruler, a hammer, and a length of string about 24cm long tied in a loop of about 16cm circumference. Experiment with balancing the ruler and hammer as in the illustration, adjusting the size of the loop if necessary. A good position for the loop is around 9cm from the end of the ruler. The fulcrum is likely to be near the 20cm mark. This sounds more complicated than it is.
- a Bible: *1 John 1:1-2*

✦ PRESENTATION
Balance the ruler on an outstretched finger – or get a volunteer to do so. Show a 2p piece and ask what will happen if you place it on the end of the balanced ruler? ... Demonstrate. ... As expected, the ruler overbalances and falls on the floor.

What happens if you move the ruler so that more sticks out one side than the other? ... Demonstrate again.

"Now what would happen if I moved the ruler along *and* hung something really heavy like this hammer from the end on the longer side? Would it balance? Of course it ... *would*!

You don't believe me? Okay, see for yourselves."

Slip on the loop of string and the hammer as in the illustration. Do it yourself first, then balance it on a child's finger to show you are not cheating. Ask the children if they would have believed it if they had not seen it for themselves.

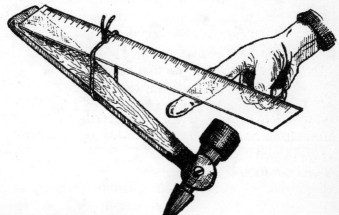

ALMOST UNBELIEVABLE

John, one of the closest friends of Jesus, once got very excited about something he had seen that was almost unbelievable. He had realized that Jesus really was the Son of God. Jesus was the meaning of life itself. And he, John, had seen him, walked with him, listened to him, and known him as a friend. He tried to get across something of the wonder of that in a letter he wrote.

Read *1 John 1:1-2*. (Please, not in a dreary 'Bible voice'. In verse 4 John says, "We write this to you so that you can be full of joy with us.")

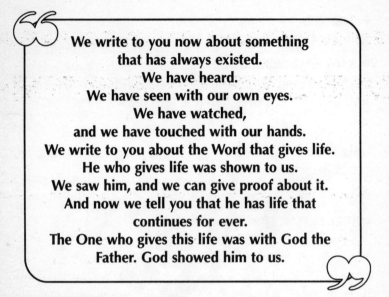

> We write to you now about something
> that has always existed.
> We have heard.
> We have seen with our own eyes.
> We have watched,
> and we have touched with our hands.
> We write to you about the Word that gives life.
> He who gives life was shown to us.
> We saw him, and we can give proof about it.
> And now we tell you that he has life that
> continues for ever.
> The One who gives this life was with God the
> Father. God showed him to us.

✦ CONCLUSION

Seeing this ruler balancing with a hammer hanging on the end is amazing. You probably need to try it yourself to convince yourself that it really works.

Seeing the things Jesus did and hearing the things he said was amazing to the people around him. His closest friends became convinced he was the Son of God. **"We saw him,"** says John, **"and we can give proof about it."**

✦ SOMETHING TO DO

Children could try this at home and show family or friends. They could tell how Jesus' friends came to believe he was the Son of God because they saw the amazing things he did with their own eyes.

ALL THE COLOURS OF WHITE

✦ THEME
Holiness is neither dull nor boring.

✦ YOU WILL NEED
- an OHP; a prism and a multi-coloured disc which appears white when spun (see if you can borrow these from a school science department); a card mask with a prism-sized cut-out
- as much colour as you can muster: children's art, posters, flowers, objects, clothes, etc.

✦ PRESENTATION
Show white light from the OHP and then make a rainbow using the prism. Introduce children to, or remind them of, some facts about light and colour. Show the reverse of the prism process by spinning a rainbow-coloured disc.

Talk about colour: brightly coloured clothes for parties or beachwear; Christmas decorations; flowers; art; etc. Talk about the effects colours have on the way we feel.

When artists paint pictures of Jesus, what colour robe is he most likely to be wearing? ... White. Why? ...

We associate white with purity, goodness, holiness. Very often we go on to think of goodness and holiness as being dull, unexciting, boring – very different from the things we associate bright colours with.

But Jesus said,

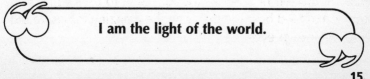

I am the light of the world.

John described Jesus in his vision like this:

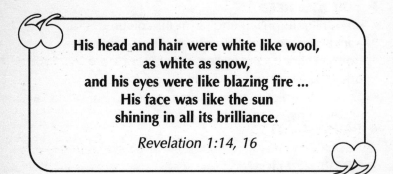

**His head and hair were white like wool,
as white as snow,
and his eyes were like blazing fire ...
His face was like the sun
shining in all its brilliance.**

Revelation 1:14, 16

Is white light colourless? No! It is all the colours of the rainbow. The Bible says that Jesus was involved in the creation of the world, so everything colourful, everything exciting, every true pleasure, was made by him and for him. Purity and holiness are not boring, they are all the riotous kaleidoscope of colour in the world spun into one dazzling white light – the light John saw in the face of Jesus.

✦ A DANCE
A group of children might prepare and perform a dance to some lively music using brightly coloured streamers.

EVERYWHERE HE WENT HE LEFT A SONG

✦ **THEME**
The compassion of Jesus.

✦ **YOU WILL NEED**
- a couple of roughly torn strips of old cloth
- a Bible: *Mark 1:40-45*
- if possible, the song *Everywhere He Went He Left a Song* from the musical **Who is this Jesus?** (see below).

✦ **PRESENTATION**
You want a volunteer, a good actor. Ask the children to put on a really sad face and choose one who does it well. Sit him/her on a chair. Wrap the cloth strips as rough bandages round his hands.

Tell how this man was ill and everyone was frightened to go near him. Talk about the effects of leprosy – feelings deadened so that when he suffered cuts or burns or accidents he did not feel any pain, and so could lose the ends of his fingers or toes or nose.

Stress that no-one would go near him, certainly not touch him, for fear of catching the disease. He had to live in a cave because people would not let him come into a town or a village. Nobody had given him a hug or a cuddle for years. Dramatise with body language.

Tell the story in *Mark 1:40-42*. When you get to, "Filled with compassion, Jesus reached out his hand and touched the man," act this out. Jesus did not have to touch him to heal him, he did it to show the man how much he cared for him.

Take off the bandages, and demonstrate how the man had

17

to go to the priest (like going to the doctor) to show that his hands were healed of the disease (v.44).

Jesus strongly warned the man not to tell anyone what had happened (v.43). Why? Because if people knew Jesus had touched a leper, they would be afraid he might have caught leprosy and not go near him. But the man was too excited to keep it a secret. He told everyone. "As a result, Jesus could no longer enter a town openly, but stayed outside in lonely places" (v.45).

Jesus' mission was to go from town to town telling people about God's kingdom. But he was prepared to put that at risk because one poor man hadn't had a hug in years and needed to feel a human touch. Fortunately, people still came to see Jesus, even outside the towns in those lonely places.

This was just one of many times Jesus healed people – and often he reached out his hand and touched them as he did so.

✦ A SONG TO LISTEN TO
Everywhere He Went He Left a Song is a song that tells how the crowds flocked to Jesus, and how he healed people of all kinds of illnesses and made them feel like singing for joy.

It is track five on the CD of the musical **Who is this Jesus?**, available from CENS at £10. (For address and further details see page 192.)

H♥LY JOKER

✦ THEME
Laughter and worshipping God can go together.

✦ PRESENTATION
Children love jokes, so why not have a 'World's Worst Joke' competition, with the winner being the one who elicits the loudest groan? Jokes should be submitted in advance, of course, or whispered first to an adult to weed out unsuitable ones!

Follow this with the story of St Philip Neri, the saint who loved a good joke. Philip started out in business, but then he had a real experience of God. He decided to live a very simple life, keeping only the barest essentials for himself. First he studied theology in Rome, and then he turned to telling other young businessmen like he had been about God.

His greatest joy was to be alone worshipping God. However, he never neglected helping people in need. But instead of doing it with a serious face, he went with a smile and a joke on his lips. Sometimes he would go around with half his beard shaved off, or dance in public. Many people came to ask his advice, from the very poorest to cardinals and kings. When an important person came, he would get someone to read a funny book to him. Perhaps that was his way of telling important people not to take themselves too seriously.

Someone wrote this verse about him:

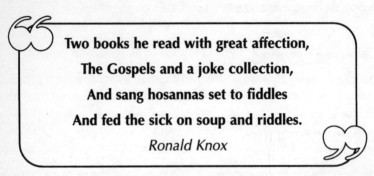

> **Two books he read with great affection,**
>
> **The Gospels and a joke collection,**
>
> **And sang hosannas set to fiddles**
>
> **And fed the sick on soup and riddles.**
>
> *Ronald Knox*

Being a Christian does not mean walking around with a long face and being a kill-joy. Philip Neri showed that you can laugh and worship God and help other people all at the same time.

By the way, who was the quickest runner ever? – Adam. He came first in the human race!

✦ TO THINK ABOUT

> **Happiness makes a person smile.**
>
> **But sadness breaks a person's spirit.**
>
> *Proverbs 15:13*

THE POINT OF PRAYER

✦ **THEME**
To consider some aspects of prayer.

✦ **YOU WILL NEED**
- a needle or pin, a match to sterilise it, and a blindfold.
- a volunteer willing to be a pin-cushion, or one who will stick pins in you!

✦ **PRESENTATION**
Blindfold your volunteer and tell the children that you are going to stick a pin in him – gently! He must say 'Ow!' as soon as he feels it and then point to the spot.

Give the obligatory sermon to the children about not doing this to each other, and sterilise the pin. Gently prick the volunteer a few times – this can be through his clothes.

Make this point: although the point of a pin is only a fraction of a millimetre across, we can instantly feel it anywhere on our body. Every cell on our body has immediate access to our brain via our network of nerves.

Now get your volunteer to stand on a chair on one leg and adopt a 'flying Superman' position. (Omit the chair if your volunteer doesn't have good balance!) It is not so immediately obvious as a pin–prick, but cells all over the body are relaying information to the brain via the nerves about the position of the limbs and weight distribution. The brain needs this information in order to send the right messages to the muscles and maintain balance. This doesn't just happen when we are trying to balance on one leg, it happens all the time. We couldn't sit, stand or walk without this information being constantly relayed to our brains.

GOD WANTS TO HEAR
Does talking to God – praying – sometimes seem a strange thing to do? It is actually very much like the messages our cells send to our brain. A tiny bit of skin half–way up your leg might not seem very important, but the instant it is touched by the point of a pin it sends a message to your brain and your brain takes notice. In the same way, every one of us, no matter how small or unimportant we feel, can send a message to God in prayer, and God will hear.

The prophet Isaiah said:

> **Surely the Lord's power is enough to save you. He can hear you when you ask him for help.**
>
> *Isaiah 59:1*

If the cells in our volunteer's body had not kept in contact with the brain, there could have been a disaster: he would have fallen off the chair. Perhaps that is one of the reasons why there are so many disasters in the world: the individual 'cells' – the people – do not realize how important it is to keep in contact with God, the Head.

✦ A PRAYER

Our Father in heaven, thank you that you always listen when we talk to you. Give us the good sense to go on talking to you and listening to you every day of our lives. We don't want to be part of a disaster! Amen.

GUIDELINES FOR GOOD COMMUNICATORS

START BY HOLDING HANDS

Much of the great teaching of Jesus springs from the moment. It starts from where people are at. Jesus takes people by the hand in their actual – but restricted – perspective and leads them a few steps to where a breathtaking vista opens up before their eyes.

The day after the 'feeding of the five thousand', for instance, the crowd catches up with Jesus on the far side of the Sea of Galilee. Clearly hoping for a repeat of the free picnic, they ask him what miraculous sign he will perform. "Our forefathers ate the manna in the desert," they say, "as it is written: 'He gave them bread from heaven to eat.'"

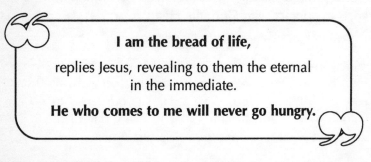

I am the bread of life,

replies Jesus, revealing to them the eternal in the immediate.

He who comes to me will never go hungry.

We must fall far short of Jesus in his gift, but we can ensure that we start from where the children are at. We can come come alongside them in their interests and concerns and lead them by the hand into a wider perspective.

Here are some examples from this section:

✦ children love humour: HOLY JOKER and KANGAROOS AND MANNA both start with different kinds of jokes.

✦ daily concerns like bullying and forgetting things provide starting points for ESCAPE and PUT A SPOON IN YOUR SHOE.

✦ children are curious and love puzzles: WITH OUR OWN EYES and A TALE OF TWO FISH begin with intriguing puzzles.

✦ many of them find the natural world fascinating: THUNDER FROM HEAVEN and BEAUTY AND THE BEAST draw on this interest.

✦ everybody enjoys stories of human behaviour outside the norm: COURAGE TO GO BLIND and UNDER THE KNIFE are two such.

PUT A SPOON IN YOUR SHOE!

✦ THEME
God helps people remember things that are important.

✦ YOU WILL NEED
- some rocks piled on a table or a copy of the illustration on OHP or paper;
- other odd things in the venue, eg poster upside–down, objects obviously out of place.
- a Bible. Check out the story in *Joshua 3* and *4:1-7* in advance.

✦ PRESENTATION
Ask for a show of hands: who has got into trouble recently for forgetting to take something to school? You might retell an incident when you forgot something yourself and the consequences.

How do people try to remember things? Write notes to themselves, perhaps – and then forget to look at them! Here is a useful tip, a way of jogging the memory: put something in the wrong place where you are bound to notice it.

For example, you need to remember to take ingredients out of the fridge for cooking tomorrow. Put a spoon in your school shoe before you go to bed! When you put the shoe on in the morning you will see – or feel – the spoon and remember the things in the fridge.

That note you have to get mum to sign? – tie your socks together. The friend you promised to call for on the way? – turn the sleeves of your jumper or anorak inside out.

It's the old knot–in–the–handkerchief principle. The important thing is to think of something you will certainly notice, and notice at the right time.

GOD DOES IT, TOO

God actually uses the same kind of trick to get people to remember important things. The difference is, he usually wants people to remember events that happened in the past.

As an example, show your stones (or picture).

This was God's spoon–in–the–shoe way of getting people to remember an exciting day in Israel's history. Briefly relate the story of the crossing of the river Jordan in *Joshua 3* and what God told Joshua to do with the stones in *4:1–7*. Future generations would see the stones and ask what they meant:

> **In the future your children will ask you, 'What do these rocks mean?'**
>
> **Tell them the Lord stopped the water from flowing in the Jordan. When the Holy Ark of the Agreement with the Lord crossed the river, the water was stopped.**
> **These rocks will help the Israelites remember this for ever.**
>
> *Joshua 4:6–8*

To finish, you might tell the children you are going to show them the stones again in the near future and see if they can remember the story.

◆ SOMETHING TO DO
Try it out and see if it works for you!

Follow–up: Victory Cup on page 231 extends the same theme.

COURAGE TO GO BLIND

✦ THEME
It takes courage to live by what we believe.

✦ YOU WILL NEED
* a blindfold; a teapot filled with cold tea or plain water; a cup; a plate and a knife; a slice of bread and a tub of margarine; a cloth to clean up with!

✦ PRESENTATION
Blindfold a volunteer. He has to imagine he is blind and is getting his tea ready. His tasks are to pour a cup of tea and to butter a slice of bread. Of course, he has to do all this by feel.

Having seen the difficulties our volunteer has got into, ask children to think what it would be like to climb a high mountain blind, a mountain with snow and ice. Ask them to suggest some of the problems and joys of such a challenge.

The highest mountain in Europe, Mont Blanc in the Alps, stands at 4807 metres. In 1988 Dave Hurst and Alan Matthews became the first blind climbers to reach the summit of Mont Blanc, a major achievement that must have given them great satisfaction.

IT TAKES COURAGE
The early Christian leader Paul seemed to view life as the same sort of exciting challenge Dave Hurst and Alan Matthews faced when they climbed Mont Blanc. He said that the mountain-top we are aiming for is heaven and what he calls 'an eternal glory'. He puts it like this:

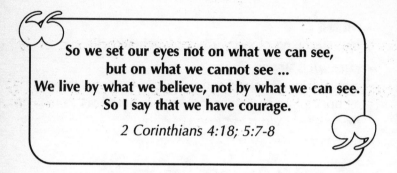

So we set our eyes not on what we can see,
but on what we cannot see ...
We live by what we believe, not by what we can see.
So I say that we have courage.

2 Corinthians 4:18; 5:7-8

It must have taken a lot of courage to climb Mont Blanc blind. It takes courage to set out on a journey when you can't see the destination. Christians believe that life is a journey and that heaven is the unseen destination. They accept the challenges and difficulties on the way, as well as the joy and excitement when they look back and see how far they have come. They believe there is going to be even greater joy when they finally make it to 'the top'.

✦ A PRAYER

Father God, help us to keep our eyes fixed on what we can't see: heaven, where you are. Give us the courage to keep going when the going gets tough. We really want to make it to the top with you! Amen.

A TALE OF TWO FISH

✦ THEME
Explaining some of the basics of Christian belief.

✦ YOU WILL NEED
- an OHP
- a drawing of a fish symbol and the Greek letters to spell ICTHUS (see illustration)
- 8 matches, cocktail sticks or similar.

I X Ø U Σ

✦ PRESENTATION
Show the fish symbol. Have children seen it on lapel-badges, the back of cars, etc.? ...

It is thought that the sign was by Christians to identify themselves to each other when they were being persecuted in Rome. The common language of the time was Greek, and the Greek word for fish was 'icthus'. The five letters that spell icthus are also the first letters of Greek words meaning: 'Jesus Christ, God's Son, Saviour'. So Christians in Rome could use the two curved lines that make a simple fish drawing as a secret sign to show they were believers in Jesus Christ.

Now for a fishy puzzle. Display the matches on the OHP arranged to make a fish as in the illustration overleaf. Ask for a volunteer to solve a puzzle. They have to move just three matches to make the fish swim in the opposite direction. The answer is shown in the illustration.

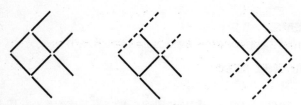

GOD GIVES THE POWER TO CHANGE

These two fish sum up the whole core of the Christian message.

First, Christians believe that God sent his Son into the world as Jesus, the Christ, the promised Messiah. He is called 'Saviour' because he came to save us from the mess we get our lives into.

What do people do when they believe that about Jesus? They turn their lives around and 'swim' in the opposite direction – God's way instead of their own way. This is an impossibly big change, but Christian experience is that God gives the power to do it.

St Paul put it like this in a letter which we have in the Bible: **"You were raised from death with Christ"** – that is to say, Jesus has become your Saviour – **" ... now put these things out of your life: bad temper, doing or saying things to hurt others, and using evil words when you talk. Do not lie to each other. You have left your old sinful life and the things you did before. You have begun to live the new life."** (*Colossians 3:1 & 8-10*) In other words, start swimming in a new direction!

✦ SOMETHING TO DO

Try the matchstick puzzle out on some friends and tell them what it means.

ESC PE

✦ **THEME**
The Christian concept of salvation

✦**YOU WILL NEED**
• metre rule or tape measure

✦ PRESENTATION
Ask children to think of a situation where they have wanted to escape. An example might be being cornered by bullies. Nature gives us many different examples of ways of escaping from danger.

Explain the meanings of the words 'predator' and 'prey' ... Animals that are preyed on by others have developed many ingenious ways of escaping. We are going to meet an animal that escapes by jumping – even though it does not have any legs!

Ask for one or two volunteers to do standing jumps and measure the distance they jump. This will provide a comparison with the exploits of the legless jumper, the fruit-fly maggot.

Fruit-fly maggots escape from possible predators such as ants by jumping enormous distances. Even though it has no legs, the maggot can jump up to thirty times its own length. If we could do that, we could do a standing jump of fifty metres!

The maggot does it by curling into a ball and gripping its rear end with a pair of mouth hooks. It then tenses its whole body with powerful muscles, lets go its rear end, and flips through the air as if fired from a catapult. It is a good job that the maggots fishermen use cannot do that!

ESCAPING FROM THE MESS

All down through history, people have felt that they needed a different kind of escape, not from some enemy but from the results of the mess they have got themselves into. Christians believe that we shall one day stand before God and be judged for what we have done in this life on earth. The early Christian leader, Paul, put it like this in one of his letters:

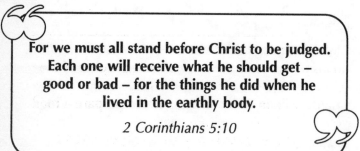

For we must all stand before Christ to be judged. Each one will receive what he should get – good or bad – for the things he did when he lived in the earthly body.

2 Corinthians 5:10

People look at themselves and ask what will happen when they face God on judgement day. They wonder how they can escape. The Bible offers a means of escape; it calls it 'salvation'. Salvation means being saved from evil or the results of sin – the wrong things we ourselves do. Christians believe this salvation came through believing in Jesus and what he has done for us.

One early Christian wrote: "How ... shall we escape if we pay no attention to such a great salvation? The Lord (Jesus) himself first announced this salvation, and those who heard him proved to us that it is true." *Hebrews 2:3*, Good News Bible.

The events of Jesus' life convinced his followers that salvation comes through him. They believed that the way to escape from sin and its consequences was being offered by God through Jesus. This is what Christians all over the world still believe today.

✦ A BIBLE PASSAGE TO THINK ABOUT

This is what John the Baptist's father said about his new baby son, looking forward to the time when John would prepare the way for Jesus and his salvation:

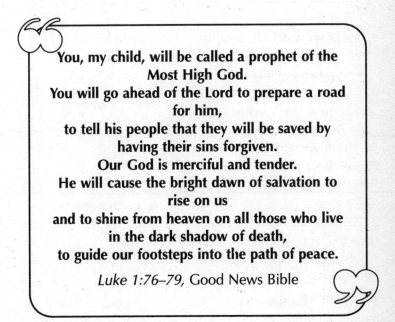

You, my child, will be called a prophet of the Most High God.
You will go ahead of the Lord to prepare a road for him,
to tell his people that they will be saved by having their sins forgiven.
Our God is merciful and tender.
He will cause the bright dawn of salvation to rise on us
and to shine from heaven on all those who live in the dark shadow of death,
to guide our footsteps into the path of peace.

Luke 1:76–79, Good News Bible

UNDER THE KNIFE

✦ THEME

Trusting God to perform 'heart' surgery.

✦YOU WILL NEED

- If anyone can perform a circus act of some kind, juggling or plate-spinning for example, that could be used as an introduction.

✦ PRESENTATION

Talk about circuses and the children's favourite acts. Include a demonstration if such is available.

Although juggling is the kind of thing anyone can try, some acts are very dangerous and should never be tried in play. One of those is knife-throwing. One lady assistant to a knife-thrower said that she had 'only' been hit three times!

Did you hear about the doctor who agreed to be a knife-thrower's target to prove how steady his nerves were? Here's the story:

Dave Flame, a professional knife thrower from Chester, had a heart problem and needed an operation. He wanted to know if the surgeon's hand was as steady with the scalpel as his was with his knives. You know what he did? He challenged the doctor to stand and have knives hurled at him. Dave reckoned he wasn't prepared to put his life in the surgeon's hands unless the surgeon was prepared to trust his life to him. And, believe it or not, Dr Peter Reid agreed.

Isn't the doctor in the story a bit like God? Christians believe we all have a kind of 'heart problem'. We all have an inner drive to do things that are stupid and hurtful. God wants to put that right. The Bible puts it like this: God says,

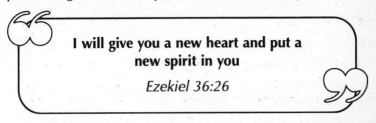

I will give you a new heart and put a new spirit in you

Ezekiel 36:26

In order for God to perform that 'heart surgery', we have to put our lives in God's hands, to trust him. For many people that is not an easy thing to do. We would rather live with the problem than risk the operation.

Would God be prepared to do what Dr Reid did, put himself at the mercy of the 'patient'? Christians believe that is what he did when Jesus came.

First, Jesus showed us what God is like.

Anyone who has seen me, has seen the Father

John 14:9

If Jesus is the kind of person you can trust, then so is God.

Second, he put his life in people's hands. But unlike Dave Flame, they couldn't be trusted. Instead of throwing knives to just miss him, they hammered nails into his wrists and into his feet and they crucified him.

This is where God did something no doctor could do. Read *Isaiah 53:4-6*.

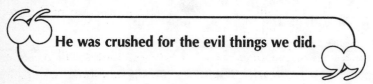

He was crushed for the evil things we did.

It is almost as if the surgeon donated his own healthy heart as a transplant for the sick patient!

Christians are people who realize that they have a heart problem and trust God as the heavenly surgeon to give them a new one. How wonderful that Jesus was prepared to put his life in our hands to prove that we can trust him completely.

✦ A PRAYER
Lord Jesus, you are better than the best doctor in the whole world. Help us to trust you completely and put our lives in your hands. Amen.

BEAUTY AND THE BEAST

✦ **THEME**
Transformation; a fresh start.

✦ **YOU WILL NEED**
• any visual focus you can find referred to below, eg video, book, picture of a dragonfly

✦ **PRESENTATION**
Most children will have seen the Disney version of *Beauty and the Beast*. Talk about the story.[1]

Beauty and the Beast is what we sometimes call a 'fairy tale'. But like many other fairty tales it has some real truth within it. There are some amazing 'beasts' which turn into 'beauties' in the natural world. One of the most dramatic transformations is that of the dragonfly. This is a real-life Beauty and the Beast story.

Like several other insects, the dragonfly spends up to the first three years of its life underwater. This part of its life-cycle is called the larval stage. At this point it is a real 'beast'. Dragonfly larvae are among the most fearsome of predators. (Explain what 'predator' means.)

The dragonfly larva preys on other insects, tadpoles, and even small fish much larger than itself. Its method of catching them is unique. The dragonfly larva has an extra-ordinarily long, folding lower jaw which ends in two large hooks. When a suitable prey is located by its rangefinder eyes, this lower jaw shoots forward in a lightning movement that takes only 1/400th of a second. Few horror films have come up with anything worse!

In midsummer the larva crawls up a reed out of the water. Its skin splits and the adult dragonfly emerges. Its crumpled wings unfold, dry and stiffen in the sun, then yesterday's monster turns into a brilliant neon tube hovering and darting over the surface of the pond.

Perhaps it is natural transformations like this that encourage us and story-tellers to believe that humans can have a real change of heart. Jesus talked about the need to be 'born again', to have a completely fresh start.

The dragonfly changes from living underwater to flying in the air. It is transformed from a beast into a beauty.

> **Christians believe that something similar can happen to people on the inside – they can be 'born again'.**

Here is how one of Jesus' followers described that transformation in a letter he wrote:

> **If anyone is in Christ, he is a new creation; the old has gone, the new has come!**
>
> *2 Corinthians 5:17,* New International Version

✦ FOLLOW-UP

Suitable follow-ups to this talk could be: Dickens' *A Christmas Carol*; Saul's conversion and adopting the new name, Paul (*Acts 22:1-21*); various drug-addicts and gangsters in *Crack in the Wall* by Jackie Pullinger (Hodder & Stoughton, 1989); other true stories of changed lives (Christian bookshops will recommend stories). Telling such a story as a serial can be very effective.

---

[1] *The Water Babies*, written by the English clergyman Charles Kingsley in 1863, is another fictional variation on the same theme.

VALUING OURSELVES

MADE OF ST★RDUST

✦ THEME
Our origin and destiny.

✦ YOU WILL NEED
- a candle, matches and a saucer. Try out the demonstration below in advance.

✦ PRESENTATION
Who is a science-fiction or Star Trek addict? ... Who has travelled to the stars in their imagination. ... Did you know that we all came from the stars, that everyone of us is made of stardust? ... **Would you like to see some stardust?**

Light a candle and hold a saucer over the flame. Show the black deposit on the saucer.

What is this? ... Carbon. Holding the saucer over the flame prevented all the carbon from burning and formed a thin layer on the saucer. This is stardust!

When a star comes near the end of its lifecycle, it throws out carbon. This dust eventually forms into planets. Every cell in our bodies contains some of that carbon. This black soot on the saucer and all the carbon in our bodies came from stars that died billions of years ago.

That is amazing to think about. Even more amazing is to think that the Bible says we shall still be alive long after our own sun has grown into a red giant, consumed the earth, and died itself. This is the promise that Jesus made in one of the best-loved verses in the Bible:

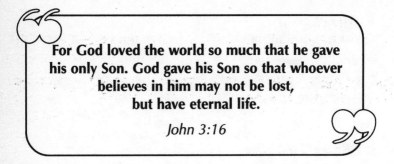

> **For God loved the world so much that he gave his only Son. God gave his Son so that whoever believes in him may not be lost, but have eternal life.**
>
> *John 3:16*

'Eternal life.' That does not mean just existing forever like a speck of stardust. It means the real you outlasting the stars in a life beyond our imagination. That is better than any sci-fi story ever written!

✦ TIME FOR REFLECTION

Play some quiet music with a science-fiction feel about it if possible. Children might like to think about what they have heard, where they have come from and where they are going to.

A L♥VEABLE TEDDY

✦ THEME
We often talk about God loving us, but tend to overlook the corollary, that we are essentially loveable (despite the loss of some of our moral stuffing!).

✦ YOU WILL NEED
- Either collect a bunch of cuddly toys or ask the children to bring in their favourites. You need one very old Teddy, obviously the worse for wear.
- A Bible: *Psalm 139*

✦ PRESENTATION
Show your soft toys one at a time, talking about them.

For fun, you could liken each one – tongue in cheek – to one of the children or adults.

Finally, bring out the old Teddy. Explain his history. He is like ... (if he's past his prime and his stuffing's coming out, he may well like you!)

Why are these soft toys like us? Because they are loveable. And we are loveable. God loves us. He doesn't just love us, he actually *likes* us. Not just when we are new, either. Some of us may be old and battered and have been in all sorts of scrapes, but that doesn't make us any the less loveable.

Psalm 139 in the Bible tells us that God planned us and knew us before we were born:

> **You saw my bones being formed as I took shape in my mother's body.**
> **When I was put together there, you saw my body as it was formed. All the days planned for me were written in your book before I was one day old.**
>
> *Psalm 139:15-16*

Like this old Teddy, God has had us around for a long time. Each one of us is an old favourite in God's collection.

✦ A PRAYER

Thank you, Lord God, for making me – not as a toy but as a real person. Help me to really know just how loveable I am to you. Amen.

ARE YOU DISPOSABLE?

✦ THEME
People may reject us, but God will not.

✦ YOU WILL NEED
- a waste-bin, preferably metal, and a selection of disposable items such as tissues, biro, razor, drink can, yoghurt pot, plastic cutlery, etc.
- a couple of figures of people cut out of paper
- a Bible: *2 Peter 3:9* and *Psalm 70*

✦ PRESENTATION
Silently use various articles – or find them unusable – and throw them away. You could start by blowing your nose and throwing the tissue in the bin, then lifting the bin on the table. Try writing with a biro which (apparently) doesn't work and throwing that away, and so on. The items should make a loud noise hitting the side of the bin if possible.

Hold up one of the paper figures and say to it (in an appropriately childish manner), **"I don't want to be friends with you any more."** Screw the figure up and throw it in the bin.

Treat another figure similarly, this time saying, **"We don't want you in the team any more. You're not good enough."**

And a third: **"We can't afford to keep you working here. I am afraid we are making you redundant."**

Talk about how hurtful it is being rejected.

We are all used to things being disposable – we throw them away when we are finished with them. Sadly, some people treat others as if they were disposable, too.

But for God, no-one is disposable. One of Jesus' disciples, Peter, explained in a letter what will happen at the end of the world. Everything that is wrong and evil in the world will be like rubbish. It will be thrown away and destroyed. People were asking then, as they do now, why God didn't do it straight away.

Peter explained it like this:

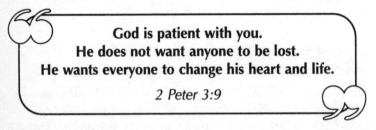

God is patient with you.
He does not want anyone to be lost.
He wants everyone to change his heart and life.

2 Peter 3:9

God does not want a single person to be lost when the evil rubbish of the world is burned. He is patiently waiting for us to allow him to clean us up and put us right. No-one is rubbish in God's sight.

Take one of the crumpled figures out of the bin and smooth it out. This is what God wants to do for us: smooth out the hurts where other people have rejected us and sort out the wrong things we have done. Then he wants to take us into his eternal life in heaven. For God, no-one is disposable.

✦ A PRAYER

Psalm 70 makes an appropriate prayer to accompany this message. It is one of David's songs when he was feeling rejected and attacked by others. It could be read by a child. Recommended version: International Children's Bible.

NAME
ABOVE ALL NAMES

✦ THEME
Our importance alongside Jesus in God's eyes.

✦ YOU WILL NEED
- a dozen or so strips of paper or card. On some write the titles of 'important people' – eg. Queen, President, Pop Star, Millionaire, Sportsman. On another card write JESUS. Leave the rest blank and have a marker pen to hand.
- a Bible: *Philippians 2:9-11* and *Ephesians 2:6*

✦ PRESENTATION
Ask the children what sort of people are important. If they come up with actual names, fit these into categories as above. Write new categories as they are suggested. Have a child hold up each category as they arise. You should end up with a line of eight or nine children holding up 'important people'.

Is there is anyone more important than all of these? ... Read *Philippians 2:9-11* – the name of Jesus "is above every name".

Ask another child to hold the card with the name JESUS on – and stand him/her on a chair so that 'JESUS' is above every other name.

Ask for two more volunteers to come and write their own names on cards. Ask the children where they think these two – and themselves – come in this group of important people. Sitting down on the floor, perhaps?

Where does God want us to be? In another letter St Paul wrote to Christians. He said that God

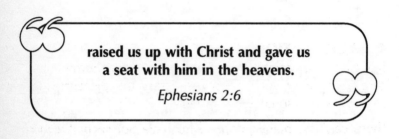

raised us up with Christ and gave us a seat with him in the heavens.

Ephesians 2:6

Stand the two children on chairs on either side of 'JESUS'. This is what God wants for us and why he sent his Son, Jesus.

Who do you think is important now?

✦ A REFLECTION
You might try this if it feels right for your group. Play some quiet music. Ask the children to close their eyes and imagine Jesus on a throne in heaven, with themselves sitting beside him. Then imagine looking down and seeing all the 'important' people way below like little ants on the earth. This is a picture of what the Bible says God wants for us.

WALLACE & GROMIT

✦ THEME
Valuing things we do and make ourselves.

✦ YOU WILL NEED
- things made by yourself or a child, eg a cake, a picture, etc., and a similar bought items

- if you can find one, a picture of Wallace and Gromit or one of their videos

✦ PRESENTATION

Talk about the relative merits of bought and home-made items and show your examples. Stress the pleasure that comes from personal achievement.

There can't be many people who have not seen *A Close Shave* by Nick Park, or his previous successes, *The Wrong Trousers* and *A Grand Day Out*. Three years running Nick won Oscars for his films – an amazing achievement.

Nick began making animated films when he was thirteen. He discovered that his dad's cine camera would take single frames – one picture at a time. The art of animation is to take one frame, move the model slightly, take another, and so on. Nick's first character was Walter the Rat, made from his mum's cotton-reels, and his first film was *Walter Goes Fishing*. It featured Walter's friend, a Plasticine worm who ended up as the bait.

Nick turned his attic at home into a studio and by the time he was fifteen had made half a dozen films. When his school found out about his talent they asked him to show the films in assembly.

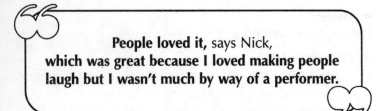

People loved it, says Nick,
**which was great because I loved making people
laugh but I wasn't much by way of a performer.**

As so often, some of Nick's talent clearly comes from his parents. Nick's dad was always out in the garden shed making things. He once made a wooden caravan and took the whole family, including five children, on holiday in Wales in it. There is clearly something of Nick's dad in Wallace, creator of the infamous techno-trousers.

"Everything was home-made," says Nick, **"my mum even made my school blazer."** At the time he wished he could have had a bought one like everyone else. Looking back he feels glad. His parents' do-it-yourself approach to life has blossomed in Nick into a talent which has made millions of people laugh.

Ask children to think about things they enjoy doing or making themselves. Or what about other members of their family? Do we sometimes think these things are not worth much because they don't seem as good as the ones we can buy in the shops?

✦ A PRAYER
God the Creator of all things, help us to feel really good about the things we do and make ourselves. Stop us when we are tempted to make fun of someone else's efforts, but help us learn how to appreciate them.   Amen.

RED FACES

✦ **THEME**
Failure is not the end of the world.

✦ **YOU WILL NEED**
- a Bible. Refresh your memory of the story of Peter's denials of Jesus in *Mark 14: 16-22*.

✦ **PRESENTATION**
"Was my face red!" "I wished I could have sunk through the floor." "I felt a right idiot." These are the kind of things we say when we have made a mess of something. It is a pretty awful feeling. Here are a few red-face stories reported in the newspapers.

- A life-sized cardboard policeman was set up in a supermarket in Ripon, North Yorkshire, to try to make people think twice about shop-lifting. Clearly it did not work, though – thieves stole the cut-out constable himself!

- The army was testing a heat-seeking anti-tank missile. An old tank was used as a target on an army firing range. Unfortunately, the test was an expensive failure. The missile missed the turret of the tank it was supposed to home in on and blew up a beer can instead!

- A man by the name of Jeffrey McLeod robbed a petrol station in Florida, America. The garage alerted the police who sent out a patrol car to give chase. We've all seen high-speed cops-and-robbers chases in films, but this one wasn't quite like that. It ended tamely when the robber's car ran out of petrol twenty miles down the road. "When you rob a gas station, you're supposed to fill the tank before you hold up the clerk," was the comment from the sheriff's office.

ONE OF THE WORST FEELINGS
We can all enjoy laughing at stories like that, but it doesn't seem so funny when we do something silly. Feeling a failure can be one of the worst feelings you can have. The question is:

Is making a mess of something the end of the world, or can we pick ourselves up and learn something from it?

Tell the story of Peter's denials of Jesus in *Mark 14:66-72*. Mark brings out Peter's feeling of shame at his failure: "He broke down and wept."

Peter could have given up then, but he didn't. After his resurrection, Jesus met Peter on the beach by the Sea of Galilee. He asked Peter three times if he loved him. Then Jesus gave Peter the job of being the leader of the first Christians, the one who was to oversee the birth of the Christian Church. Jesus helped Peter put his failure behind him and go on to do great things.

✦ A PRAYER

First, a moment of quiet to think about anything we have made a mess of and feel bad about.

Father in heaven, help us not to feel so bad about our mistakes that we give up. Show us how to learn from our mistakes and go on to greater things. Amen.

GUIDELINES FOR GOOD COMMUNICATORS

THE ILLUSTRATION IS THE MESSAGE

"The Lord is my shepherd," said David unforgettably. He did not start with a five-point abstract treatise on the nature of God and then throw in an illustration to help the slower-of-mind get the point. The illustration *was* the message.

The death of Jesus is the pivot of Christianity. Yet Jesus gave hardly any teaching about the meaning of his death. He simply took a piece of Passover bread and said, "This is my body." Then he took a cup of wine and said, "This is my blood".

When you get the picture, you've got the message.

It is not easy for Western-educated minds to put their faith in the power of the picture (which is strange considering we have been brought up with the matchless examples given above). And yet we are told that society is moving strongly in the direction of the image being more important than the word. This is the world our children live in. We had better learn how to use the image before we get left behind.

At the very least we can endeavour not to underestimate the place of illustrations in the talks we give to children. Take two examples from this section, A LOVEABLE TEDDY and ARE YOU DISPOS-ABLE? In each case there is a strong image. It is that image which is likely to remain in the minds of the children even if our explanations make little impact.

Seek out strong illustrations like these. After all, it is the Biblical way.

TIMELESS VIRTUES

BE AN ENCOURAGER!

◆ THEME
Encouraging one another.

◆ YOU WILL NEED
- a radio
- a globe, if possible.

◆ PRESENTATION
Switch on the radio and move the tuning along the medium or short wave band to pick up some foreign stations.

Do children know who made many of the discoveries that enable us to send and receive radio signals? ...

His name was Marconi. It sounds like 'macaroni' – so can anyone guess which country he came from? ... Italy. However, although he was Italian, many of his famous and successful experiments were carried out in England. We are going to find out why.

Who likes doing experiments with batteries and wires and light bulbs? ... So did Marconi, except that he did not have light bulbs to experiment with because they hadn't been invented then! He was born in 1874. One thing fascinated him. If you made a spark in one electrical circuit it caused a small amount of electricity to flow in another wire nearby, one that was not connected to the first circuit at all. It was as though the first circuit was sending a signal to the second circuit. How did that happen? It was *wire-less* communication.

Young Marconi started to do some experiments to see if he could find out what was happening. The trouble was, he got little encouragement to continue with them in Italy. He moved to England, and there he did find the encouragement he needed.

In 1896 he demonstrated the possibilities by sending signals four miles across Salisbury Plain in southern England. Later that year, he sent signals nine miles across the Bristol Channel.

That was certainly interesting, but people thought that the distance signals could be sent and received would be limited by the earth's curve – the radio waves travelled in a straight line and would go off into space. Then, in December 1901, Marconi sent a signal from Cornwall which was received right across the Atlantic Ocean in St John's, Newfoundland. (Show on the globe.) That caused a worldwide sensation.

> **Imagine, when the fastest means of communication was the time it took a steamboat to carry a letter, suddenly discovering that a message could be sent thousands of miles instantaneously.**

In 1909 Marconi was awarded the Nobel Prize for Physics.

All our modern TV and radio flows from that. What might have happened if nobody had encouraged Marconi in England either? He might have given up. It might have been years before someone else got as curious. We might still be watching TV in black and white!

Geniuses and inventors and top sports men and women take the headlines, but behind them are the encouragers, the ones who have faith in them and help them carry on when things go wrong. Not everyone can be a genius, but anyone can be an encourager.

A FAMOUS ENCOURAGER

One of the most famous men in the Bible is Paul, who took the Christian message to large parts of the Roman Empire. He had a friend who first introduced him to the leaders of the early Church, and then went with him on some of his journeys. We only hear this man's real name – Joseph – once (*Acts 4:36*). The rest of the time he is called by his nickname, Barnabas. Guess what that means? – **The Encourager.**

> **How do you become a Barnabas The Encourager?**

By saying things like: "That looks really great". Or: "You've done a good job there". Or: "I think you can do it. Go for it!" Or: "Try it, I'll give you a hand".

One of the rewards of being an encourager is the smiles of thanks you get. And then, you never know, you might just be helping a Marconi or a Paul or a future England player along the road to some really great achievement! Go for it!

✦ SOMETHING TO DO

Make a 'Barnabas' badge. Award it in a week's time to someone who is nominated as the week's best encourager. That way we can encourage each other to be encouragers!

FORMATION FLYING

✦ THEME
Lessons from nature about supporting one another in a team.

✦ YOU WILL NEED
- a picture of some geese, if possible

✦ PRESENTATION
Who has seen film of geese flying in a V-formation? ... Who has seen them in real life? ... Does anyone know why they fly like that? ... It gives them several advantages. We can learn some valuable lessons from them.

First, as each bird flaps its wings, the air currents it creates help the bird immediately behind it. So each goose except the lead bird uses less effort and can fly further. Cyclists racing together as a team get a similar effect. If one goose on its own could fly 100 miles, geese together in V-formation could fly 171 miles!

Lesson number 1 – *work together as a team, you go a lot further.*

Second, as the lead goose gets tired, another takes its place. By taking it in turns to lead they share the load. No-one drops out through exhaustion.

Lesson number 2 – *share out the load so that we all make it to our goal together.*

Third, if one goose has to drop out because it gets sick or is wounded by someone shooting at it, two other geese leave the formation and follow it down to help and protect it.

They stay with the hurt goose until it can fly again.

Lesson number 3 – *we are always glad of somebody sticking by us if we get hurt. Are we ready to do the same for others?*

Fourth, if you have seen geese flying like this, you will know that they honk as they fly. It is the geese at the back who honk. They do it to let the leaders know they are following and keeping up. Anyone who has played hockey or football knows how much it helps when the team shout encouragement to one another. That is true whatever sort of group we are in.

Lesson number 4 – *saying things like, "That's really good", makes people feel happier and work better. The whole group or team benefits.*

Did you ever hear anyone called a 'silly goose'?

It seems geese aren't that silly at all.
In fact, there are a lot of very sensible lessons we can learn from them.

✦ **A PRAYER**

Lord God, Jesus told people to
"look at the birds in the air".
Help us to take that advice and learn some lessons
that will help us to go a lot further in life.
Amen.

Adapted from an article by Nigel Lee in the UCCF newsletter, Fellowship Link. Used by permission.

MOTHER'S DAY PET

✦ THEME
Appreciating what our Mothers do for us.

✦ YOU WILL NEED
- a large cardboard box with a hole cut in the back for your forearm to go into the box. Punch a couple of holes in the lid and tie with string so that it does not come open until you are ready.
- a hand-mirror inside the box.

✦ PRESENTATION
Talk about pets and say you have a very unusual and special pet who needs a new owner. Show the box. Your arm is inside, but this is hidden from the children. Make scratching and movement noises inside the box.

Explain that looking after this pet is very demanding. Ask for a volunteer. Go through the details below slowly. Keep asking your volunteer if she is prepared to go to this much trouble. If she backs out at any point, ask for another volunteer to take her place.

When this pet is young it needs feeding six to eight times a day, including in the middle of the night. (**"Could you do that?"**...) It also makes a nasty smelly mess that has to be cleaned up ... and it needs bathing every day.

As it gets a bit bigger, you have to spend a lot of time talking to it, playing with it and taking it for walks. It is also quite mischievous and can make quite a mess of your things if it is left to itself.

WORRY AND SLEEPLESS NIGHTS

This stage lasts several years, and all the time it is growing. As it gets older, it will quite likely get into trouble sometimes and cause you lots of worry and sleepless nights. Eventually it will grow as big as you are.

Then there is the cost. Feeding this pet and giving it all the other things it needs costs as much as £3000 per year. **Can you afford it?** ...

Children being as optimistic as they are, you should end up with a volunteer who is prepared to say 'yes' to all this. Tell her you are going to let her see this special pet now. Ask her just to look at it, but not say anything. Open the lid and hold the mirror at an angle inside the box so she can see her own face, but the other children cannot see the mirror. (Practise this at home with a member of the family.) Enjoy the expression on her face!

Now show the rest of the children the mirror. For those who are slow to catch on, explain how all you have said applies to them. Very few of them would really want to take on the responsibility of looking after a 'pet' like that, but that is what their mums have done.

Commandment number five of the Ten Commandments says:

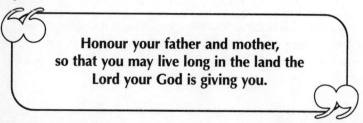

**Honour your father and mother,
so that you may live long in the land the
Lord your God is giving you.**

Realising what a big job it is looking after a child helps us understand why it is good to honour our mums on Mother's Day.

✦ A PRAYER

A group of children might be asked in advance to prepare some prayers for their mums. Or perhaps we should pray to be the least difficult pets possible!

GUIDELINES FOR GOOD COMMUNICATORS

GET THEM INVOLVED

When we have a talk to prepare, let's ask ourselves, "Am I treating the children as just an audience – literally 'hearers' only – or am I inviting them to be active participants?" The latter leads to far more effective communication.

One way of making them active participants is to actually involve one or two, as in MOTHER'S DAY PET or GIVING AND RECEIVING. This effects the whole group, not just the chosen volunteers. The other children identify with their friends out the front and think how they would react if it was them.

If you want to know how to milk this effect for all it's worth, watch a few TV game or quiz shows and pick up some tips. A good game show host gets terrific involvement from the audience. Of course, the one thing we should never do with a child volunteer is to make him or her a victim of ridicule.

Another way of getting active involvement is to raise a question in the minds of the children. SWIMMING AGAINST THE CURRENT does this: everyone wants to know what the dead fish is there for. Similarly in MOTHER'S DAY PET, the desire to know what this strange creature is in the box keeps everyone on the edge of their seats. It is the kind of technique the prophet Ezekiel used to great effect (see Ezekiel 4 and 5 for some dramatic examples).

Involving children in these ways (and in others in this volume) opens mental doors and increases receptivity to the messages we want to convey.

GORILLAS AND ALIENS

✦ **THEME**
The Bible shows us how to treat people who are different from us.

✦ **YOU WILL NEED**
- A picture of a gorilla if you can find one.
- Some children could be given the Bible verses to read.

✦ **PRESENTATION**
Find out which children have seen gorillas at a zoo or on TV. Show a picture if you have one.

One toddler in a pushchair had his first experience of a gorilla at Twycross Zoo in Warwickshire. The toddler was looking through the massive glass window which forms one wall of the gorillas' pen when a large male raced up and flung himself against the glass. The child concentrated for a moment to find words to describe the frightening incident. "Big monkey," he said solemnly. "Dang'rous!"

In the spring of 1996, another small boy suffered a much more serious experience. The three-year old (his parents asked for his name not to be released) was on an outing to Brookfield Zoo in Illinois, America. He climbed over some railings and fell six metres onto a concrete floor of an enclosure which was home to seven gorillas. You can imagine his parents' horror seeing their son lying unconscious on the ground below them. **What would the gorillas do?**

The first one to approach the limp body was eight-year old Binti Jua, a mother with her own infant. Her name is Swahili

71

for 'Daughter of Sunshine'. With her baby on her back, Binti Jua picked up the unconscious boy and carried him to the door of the pen. She handed him over to waiting first-aiders who were able to look after him and call an ambulance. While she was doing this, keepers sprayed the other gorillas with water to keep them back.

For a gorilla, a human is another species, a sort of alien. What prompted Binti Jua to rescue a human child? Was it maternal instinct? Was it because she herself had been raised by humans? (She had to be taught how to look after her own baby.) Unfortunately, she cannot talk to tell us.

When we look at how human beings treat other humans who are different from them, it seems that we need to be taught the right way to do it. Perhaps that is why there are lots of rules in the early chapters of the Bible on how to treat 'aliens'. 'Aliens' are strangers, people who look different or talk differently to us.

Some of God's rules say that aliens should be treated fairly:

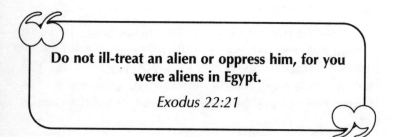

Do not ill-treat an alien or oppress him, for you were aliens in Egypt.

Exodus 22:21

> **The community is to have the same rules for you and for the alien living among you. ... You and the alien shall be the same before the Lord.**
>
> *Numbers 15:15*

Other rules were meant to make sure strangers or foreigners without jobs had enough to eat in the days when there were no shops:

> **Do not go over your vineyard a second time or pick up the grapes that have fallen. Leave them for the poor and the alien. I am the Lord your God.**
>
> *Leviticus 19:10*

> **When you reap the harvest of your land, do not reap to the very edges of your field or gather the gleanings of your harvest. Leave them for the poor and the alien. I am the Lord your God.**
>
> *Leviticus 23:22*

Strangers are not to be left out when there are meetings – or even parties!

> **Assemble the people - men, women and children, and the aliens living in your towns - so that they can listen [to the law].**
>
> *Deuteronomy 30:12*

> **Be joyful at your Feast - you, your sons and daughters, ... the aliens, the fatherless and the widows who live in your towns.**
>
> *Deuteronomy 16:14*

These rules were written for people who lived very different kinds of lives to ours. But it is very clear how God wants us to treat aliens or strangers: we should treat them the same as us, look after their needs, and make sure they don't get left out. Do we need a gorilla to teach us a lesson to do that?

✦ SOMETHING TO DO
Draw up a list of 'rules' on how to make someone welcome who has just moved into your street or your class.

SWIMMING AGAINST THE CURRENT

✦ **THEME**

Drifting with the crowd is not really living.

✦ **YOU WILL NEED**

- a whole dead fish (from a fish shop)
- a Bible: *Matthew 7:13-14*

If possible, suspend the fish on a length of string so that it hangs in the air at the front of the room, preferably a foot or two above your head. This will intrigue the children and ensure their close attention.

✦ **PRESENTATION**

Begin by standing under the fish, but do not acknowledge it or make any reference to it. This adds to the intrigue.

Talk about the kind of temptations that can arise when people just drift with the crowd. Relate to any specific local or topical issues, eg bullying, shop-lifting, vandalism.

Ask the children if they have seen film of salmon swimming up-river to breed. Pictures of the great fish leaping into the air as they try to climb waterfalls are very impressive. Sometimes they have to try again and again to fight their way through rocks and against powerful currents. This is life at full stretch.

Now compare that picture with the dead fish. Dead fish don't do much – just hang around! They float downstream and decay, instead of leaping up waterfalls.

Real life is often a question of swimming upstream, against the current and the opposite way to dead fish floating past.

Jesus once painted a similar kind of picture. In his picture it wasn't fish in a river, but people on two different kinds of roads. He said:

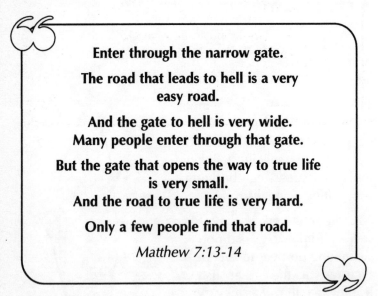

Enter through the narrow gate.

The road that leads to hell is a very easy road.

**And the gate to hell is very wide.
Many people enter through that gate.**

**But the gate that opens the way to true life is very small.
And the road to true life is very hard.**

Only a few people find that road.

Matthew 7:13-14

It seems like we have a choice in life. One way is tough and sometimes lonely, but exciting. It leads to finding out what life is all about. The other way is easy, just drifting with the crowd, but it ends in shame and disappointment and misery.

Which sort of fish do you want to be?

✦ A PRAYER

This prayer is by David, the shepherd boy who became a king:

> **Lord, tell me your ways.**
> **Show me how to live.**
> **Guide me in your truth.**
> **Teach me, my God, my Saviour.**
> **I trust you all day long.**
>
> *Psalm 25:4-5*

Original idea by David Smith.

UNSELFISH CLOCKWORK

✦ THEME
The contrast between selfishness and being ready to help others.

✦ YOU WILL NEED
- a wind-up toy or alarm-clock

✦ PRESENTATION
Show your clockwork toy or set the alarm-clock ringing. Discuss with the children the relative merits of powering toys and clocks by clockwork or by batteries.

Now think if you lived in a village in Africa with no mains electricity, a long walk to the nearest shop, and very little money. Would clockwork or batteries be best?

People who live in African villages might not put toys or clocks very high on the list of things they would like to own.

One thing many people do want is a radio.

And some of the information they could listen to on a radio might save their lives. There are lots of things they could learn which would help them to avoid catching diseases. One of Africa's greatest disasters is the spread of Aids. If more people had radios, governments and health workers could get vital information to them and save people from getting infected.

But radios need batteries. Or do they?

Inventor Trevor Baylis saw TV reports on Aids in Africa and started thinking about how to make a radio that doesn't need mains electricity or batteries. Winding up a spring to power a clock or a watch or a toy has long been used as a way of storing energy and releasing it slowly.

Could a clockwork spring run a mini-generator and make enough electricity to power a radio?

Trevor Baylis started experimenting and managed to make it work.

His original model was shown on *Tomorrow's World*. There were still lots of problems, but a businessman liked the idea, and money was found to explore it further. In the end they succeeded in making a radio which gives forty minutes listening from twenty seconds winding.

A company called BayGen built a factory in South Africa to produce the new Freeplay radios. They employ handicapped people on the production line making thousands of radios every month. Aid agencies are buying the radios to give away to people who could not get information any other way.

Trevor Bayliss could have been selfish with his talent for inventing things. Instead, he used it to help others. James (who was probably one of Jesus' brothers) wrote about this in a letter in the Bible.

> **Where there is jealousy and selfishness, there will be confusion and every kind of evil.**

How different this is from people who have real wisdom that is

> **... always ready to help those who are troubled and to do good for others. This wisdom is always fair and honest.**
>
> *James 3:16-17*

Some people in the Third World now have the voices on Trevor's clockwork radios to warn them of the dangers of Aids and other diseases.

> **We all have a little voice built into our heads to warn us of the dangers of selfishness.**
>
> **It doesn't need either batteries or a spring.**
>
> **It is called our 'conscience'.**

✦ A PRAYER

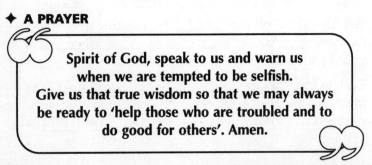

> **Spirit of God, speak to us and warn us when we are tempted to be selfish. Give us that true wisdom so that we may always be ready to 'help those who are troubled and to do good for others'. Amen.**

THE 'UGH' JOBS

✦ THEME
Serving others.

✦ YOU WILL NEED
- a bowl, water, soap and towel.
- prepare the story of Jesus washing the disciples' feet in *John 13:1-20*

✦ PRESENTATION
Ask for two volunteers and ask one to wash the other one's feet. Hopefully the other children will go, 'ugh'.

Tell the story of *John 13:1-20*, including the following explanations. Ask the children to go 'ugh' when you raise your hand.

Explain how the disciples' feet were dirty and smelly ('ugh') from all the walking where the pollution was not car exhausts but donkey and camel droppings (ugh). When you ate your dinner you lay out on a couch and someone else's feet were in your face ('ugh') – that was not very nice when they were dirty and smelly ('ugh'). Slaves washed people's feet which was an ('ugh') job.

> **But in this story there are no slaves, so who is going to wash the disciples' feet? Jesus did, and Jesus said we should do the same.**

Not literally – these days we usually wear shoes and socks instead of sandals and we do not have camels. Rather it means that we should think of others as better than ourselves, not be afraid to do the dirty jobs and the boring jobs.

Children might be asked to suggest what some of these jobs might be, both at school and at home. ... **Who usually does those jobs?**

The foot-washer knelt at the feet of the person he washed. Jesus set his disciples an example by doing it for them.

> **Are we willing to serve others and do some of the 'ugh' jobs?**

✦ REFLECTION AND RESPONSE
A moment for each one to think of a particular job he or she could offer to do today, perhaps something at home.

Original idea by Malcolm Rogers of Ipswich.

PEOPLE OR OBJECTS

✦ THEME
Treating others as people, not as objects.

✦ YOU WILL NEED
- a stone or a piece of wood
- a pot-plant
- a doll
- a piece of carpet to protect the floor

✦ PRESENTATION
Hold up the stone or piece of wood and drop it on the mat.
(Make sure it is far enough away from children not to bounce and hit anyone.)

Ask if anyone thinks that is wrong, or if the stone will object to being dropped? ... No, of course not.

Now hold up the pot-plant. If you drop that, would that be wrong? ...

It would certainly cause a mess; the plant might die, but could probably be repotted and survive. Would anyone call the police? ... Could you be imprisoned for plant-abuse?

Hold up the doll. Ask children to imagine it is a real baby. Would it be wrong to drop a baby? ...

Would anyone think they ought to call the police or social services? ...

NAME CALLING
Pick up the stone and start calling it names, eg:

"What a miserable, ugly little pebble you are! I'd rather spend my holidays on the town rubbish dump than sit on a beach with you. ...

If you were inside a volcano it would erupt just to spew you out."

That may be rather stupid, but is it doing any harm? ...

Now insult one of the children (one with a good self-image) or an imaginary person. Eg:

"Have you looked in a mirror lately – or are you too much of a coward? ...

Quick, put a helmet on your head! Here comes a wood-pecker!" ...

If those comments were serious, would that do any harm?

Is there a difference between insulting a stone and a person?

Talk about how we can treat people as less than human – as objects – whenever we fail to consider their feelings. There is all the difference in the world between kicking a ball and kicking a person:

In a letter in the Bible, Paul gives some guide-lines on how to treat each other. Here is what he says:

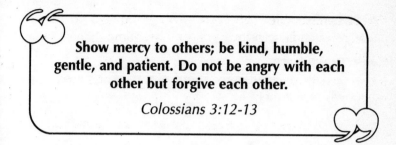

> **Show mercy to others; be kind, humble, gentle, and patient. Do not be angry with each other but forgive each other.**
>
> *Colossians 3:12-13*

God always treats us as people, people he loves, not as objects. He calls on us to treat each other in the same way. You can't be kind, gentle or patient with a stone! But you can be kind to someone else.

✦ A PRAYER

> **Lord God, you know how much we hate it when people are unkind to us and treat us as objects. Help us never to do that to other people. Amen.**

GIVING & RECEIVING

✦ THEME
God rewards generosity.

✦ YOU WILL NEED
- a packet of Smarties or thirty other small sweets; two bowls to put them in.
- a Bible: *Mark 4:24*

✦ PRESENTATION
Ask for one volunteer (A), then choose one other (B) who would not be among A's circle of friends.

Give both volunteers an empty bowl and count ten Smarties into A's bowl.

Tell A he can keep them all for himself **or**

give just one to B **or**

give as many to B as he wants.

He must decide and do it straight away.

When he has done so, say you have twenty Smarties left and you are going to give A the same proportion of your twenty as he gave of his ten to B.

Explain this carefully to the whole group and illustrate what would happen in different cases. Eg if A gave B one, you give A two of yours; if A gave B all of his, you give all yours to A. How ever many are left of your twenty, you are going to give those to B.

Give A the correct proportion, then give the rest of the twenty to B. Comment on how A has done well or badly out of this depending on his generosity to B in the first place.

Read *Mark 4:24.* Jesus said,

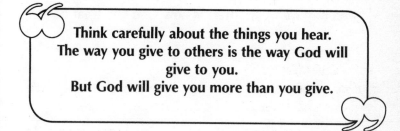

Think carefully about the things you hear.
The way you give to others is the way God will give to you.
But God will give you more than you give.

In other words, if we are generous to others, God will be generous to us. If we are mean to others God will be mean to us. And as God has far more to give than we ever have, it is a very good thing to be on the receiving end of God's generosity!

That does not mean that if we give half our bar of chocolate away today we can automatically expect a whole chocolate bar to drop out of the sky tomorrow!

God rewards the truly generous spirit, and he may give back to us in quite different ways to the way we have given.

Jesus repeated this kind of thing several times. Clearly, he saw this as one of the basic rules of living:

the way we treat others is how God will treat us.

✦ A PRAYER

Give me a truly generous spirit, Lord God.
When I am tempted to be selfish, remind me
that you will treat me in the same way as
I treat others. Amen.

GOOD AND BAD CHOICES

MAKING CHOICES

✦ **THEME**

We can ask God to help us when we have difficult choices to make.

✦ **YOU WILL NEED**

- a large bar of chocolate or other prize
- three envelopes with red, blue and yellow stickers or felt-tip marks on them; three pieces of paper with these words written on them and sealed in the envelopes:

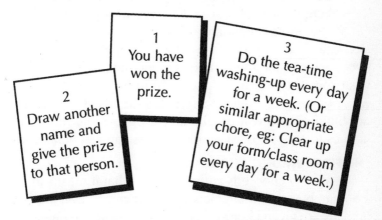

1
You have won the prize.

2
Draw another name and give the prize to that person.

3
Do the tea-time washing-up every day for a week. (Or similar appropriate chore, eg: Clear up your form/class room every day for a week.)

- a large sheet of paper or card with some black ticks and red crosses drawn on (more ticks than crosses) as in the illustration
- the names of a few children on slips of paper in a hat or box.

✦ **PRESENTATION**

Show the prize and explain that you are going to draw a name from the hat. This person is going to get a chance to win the prize. Draw the name and bring the child to the front. Show the three envelopes and explain what is written on slips inside (as above). Let him choose one. He either gets the prize, draws another name to give it to, or promises to do whatever the chore is. There should be people eager to ensure he keeps his promise!

Continue like this: We all make scores of choices every day. Some are very ordinary, such as whether to have lasagne or a beefburger for lunch, or which TV programme to watch. Some are more important: who to be friends with, for example. As we get older the choices we make for ourselves become more and more important. we shall have to choose what sort of job to train for, where to live, who to go out with or marry. Unlike the three envelopes, most choices are not blind. There will usually be people or information to help us to choose. Even so, big choices can feel quite risky.

THE FIRST WRONG CHOICE
Being able to choose is at the heart of what it means to be a human being. In the Bible story of Adam and Eve, the first humans are given choices. They get to choose the names of all the animals. They can choose from lots of different fruits that are good to eat. There is just one fruit that is harmful to them. We know the story: eventually they choose the one thing they were told not to do. The consequences are very serious.

Show the sheet with the ticks and crosses on it. The ticks stand for good choices, the crosses for bad choices. Some of the crosses stand for things that parents, teachers and others have told us are can harm us. Every one of us makes mistakes and gets a cross sometimes. But we can pray and ask God to help us make good choices. After all, he is the only one who knows what the results of our choice will be.

✦ A PRAYER
Father in Heaven, you know everything. I don't want to make the same kind of mistake Adam and Eve made. Help me to select from all the good choices in life you have given me. Help me to hear that small voice inside that warns me when I am about to make a mistake. Amen.

GUIDELINES FOR GOOD COMMUNICATORS

VISUALISE IT!

Look at UP IN SMOKE on page 103. The basis of this talk is a few figures found in one news item and a quote from another. Given as a straight talk it would be fairly dull. The trick with this sort of material is to ask, 'How can I translate some of the elements visually?'

The key element here is: *5.7 billion tons of carbon going up in smoke each year.* Where do we find carbon in a form that children will be familiar with? A little thought turns up the answer: in barbecue charcoal. If there isn't a bag in the garage already, one can soon be picked up. Some elementary maths translates tons into bags, but it is such a large number as to be almost meaningless. Writing it onto a roll of paper and slowly unrolling it for dramatic effect creates the necessary impact.

Copying the quote, "They didn't pay God's creation enough respect," on to OHP acetate adds a further visual element and helps reinforce the key teaching.

Another example is in 1 IN 14 MILLION in the DON'T GET CAUGHT section. Visualising the chance of winning the lottery as the same as finding one 10p coin in a pile 26 km high is staggering. I had to repeatedly run the figures through a calculator and ask a mathematician to check them before I could convince myself it was true!

The principle is simple and well-known, but too often forgotten. Yet the time spent in thought and preparation is repaid many times over by the impact made. Visualise it!

THE RIGHT CHOICE ✔

✦ THEME
An example of making a good choice.

✦ YOU WILL NEED
- a Bible. Prepare to retell the story in in *1 Samuel 24* in your own words.
- the sheet with black ticks and red crosses on it from MAKING CHOICES.

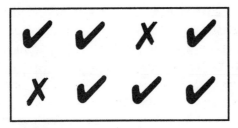

✦ PRESENTATION
Show the ticks and crosses and remind children of the importance of making good choices. Adam and Eve made a bad choice when they chose the one fruit God had told them not to eat. Here is a story about a famous man and how he made a good choice one day.

After David defeated Goliath he became a national hero and King Saul became so jealous that he tried to kill David. David drew a bunch of outlaws around him, but was pursued by Saul and his army. Sometimes the outlaws had to hide in caves to escape.

Relate the story of David choosing to spare Saul's life as recounted in *1 Samuel 24.*

Finish with Saul's words in verses 19-20:

> If a man finds his enemy, he won't send
> him away with goodness, will he?
> May the Lord reward you because you were good
> to me today. I know you will surely be king.
> You will rule the kingdom of Israel.

This came true some time later. Saul was killed in a battle against the Philistines. The people all chose David as the new king of Israel. David had chosen to do the right thing, and God rewarded him.

✦ SOMETHING TO THINK ABOUT

How many of us have said to somebody recently, "I'll get my own back on you!"? We may even have imagined the nasty things we would like to do to that person. How about deciding to choose *not* to get our own back. Remember how God rewarded David when he chose to do the right thing.

THE SECRET OF BEING HAPPY

✦ THEME
To illustrate the meaning of the Tenth Commandment: Do not covet.

✦ YOU WILL NEED
- four sheets of paper with pictures like those below on one side and readings on the other. Rehearse four readers.

✦ PRESENTATION

The four children stand in a row, hold up their papers, and read in succession.

CHILD 1 I'm off to take my dog for a walk in the park. I can see some lovely gardens with their own tennis-courts in them. I'd love to live in one of those houses.

(Picture 1)

CHILD 2 I live in a big house near the park. I sit by the window most of the day watching the people go by. Look! There's a man jogging. I'd love to do that.

(Picture 2)

CHILD 3 I've nearly finished my three-mile jog. I'm so hungry. I'd love some fish and chips, but I haven't any money to buy some.

(Picture 3)

CHILD 4 I'll buy some fish and chips then go home to my flat. There will be no-one there. I'm so lonely. I'd love to have a friend, or even a cat or a dog like that girl in the park

(Picture 4)

Leader Thank you for reading so well. Don't go away yet because we shall need you again.

So often we look at other people and want what they have: sweets at playtime, a new football, some new trainers. But other people look at us and want what we have. Let's experiment. Would our readers now reverse the order – number 4 read first. Turn and look at the next person when you finish.

CHILD 4 I'll just eat my fish and chips. I'm getting a bit fat. I wish I were fit like that man jogging.

CHILD 3 I'll jog past this big house where that pretty girl sits in the window. She looks terrific. I wish she were my girlfriend.

CHILD 2 There's that girl again, walking her dog in the park I wish I could get up and go for a walk, not have to sit in this wheelchair all day.

CHILD 1 Come on, dog. Why does my mum make me take you for a walk every day? It's not fair. I wish I could live on my own in my own flat like that lady over there.

LEADER We are never satisfied, are we? We always want what somebody else has. It's like a chain going round and round.

In the Bible St Paul says,

> **I have learned the secret of being happy at any time in everything that happens.**
>
> *Philippians 4:12*

You might be thinking, 'That's okay for Paul, he was a saint. You don't know how tough my life is.'

Actually, Paul's life was pretty tough. Several times he got badly beaten up or thrown into prison. His secret was that he knew God was with him all the time and nothing else was as important as that. He chose to think about that, rather than thinking how badly done to he was.

✦ SOMETHING TO THINK ABOUT

As we finish, let's have a moment of quiet. Think of something you have that someone else might like – even if it is just being able to walk and run – and say thank you for that. Ask God to help you choose to be thankful for what you have, rather than wanting what someone else has.

By Pat Gutteridge, co-author of *52 Ideas for Junior Classroom Assemblies* (Monarch, 1995).

ACTIONS SPEAK LOUDER THAN WORDS

✦ **THEME**

What we do is more important than what we say.

✦ **PRESENTATION**

Ask children what they would think if someone came to their school to present a special lesson on how to survive in the wild but had to be rescued himself before the lesson could begin?

This happened in October 1992 at Allhallows School in Devon. The school is in a beautiful part of the country, right on the clifftops overlooking the sea. The visiting speaker, Mr Alistair Emms, arrived early and decided to go for a walk before his talk on survival techniques. When he hadn't returned an hour later, staff at the school began to fear for his safety.

Allhallows is a very unusual school. All round the shores of Britain there are coastguards who keep a watch out for people in difficulty. Allhallows is the only school in the country to have its own Auxiliary Coastguard Unit. This group of staff and pupils was mobilized to go off in search of Mr Emms, but they could not find any trace of him. Other coastguard units were then called, plus the police. The search party now numbered forty local people, five police officers, one tracker dog, and two helicopters!

Five hours later, a team scaling an inaccessible cliff face and cutting their way through bushes finally heard cries for help. They found Mr Emms on a ledge. Although he had only a groundsheet with him, and no food, he then told his rescuers he wanted to stay there!

A policeman said; "It's all a bit weird, but basically he just wanted to stay there and come down when he was ready. Eventually he was talked into getting into the helicopter."

The school decided not to invite Mr Emms back to give the lesson on survival which he had failed to deliver.

SAYING AND DOING

Which is more important: what we say or what we do? For example, who does more for the environment: the person who designs an eye-catching poster or the one who actually picks up the litter and turns off the lights?

Jesus put it like this in a simple story ending with a question:

> **Now what do you think? There was once a man who had two sons. he went to the elder one and said, 'Son, go and work in the vineyard today.' 'I don't want to,' he answered, but later he changed his mind and went. Then the father went to the other son and said the same thing. 'Yes, sir,' he answered, but he did not go. Which of the two did what his father wanted?**
>
> *Matthew 21:28-31a*, Good News Bible

An old saying goes, 'Actions speak louder than words.' The search party and people who read the story in the newspaper judged Mr Emms by what he did, not by whatever he might have said in his talk. Jesus' story shows us that God judges us in the same way. Perhaps we might pray for our actions to match the best of our words.

This story appeared in *The Independent*, 14.10.92.

UP IN SMOKE

♦ **THEME**
The need to co-operate with the Creator in order to clean up the world.

♦ **YOU WILL NEED**
- a bag of barbecue charcoal
- a roll of paper with one of these numbers printed in large letters:
  for a 5kg bag of charcoal, **1,140,000,000,000**;

  for a 3kg bag, **1,710,000,000,000**.

♦ **PRESENTATION**
Show a lump of charcoal. Talk about what it is made of – largely carbon. Explain about the gas that is produced when it is burned – carbon dioxide.

When we burn charcoal or fossil fuels such as coal or oil, much of the carbon goes into our atmosphere as carbon dioxide, a greenhouse gas. Some of the carbon may not burn but literally 'go up in smoke' as tiny specks of black soot.

How much carbon do we put into the atmosphere each year, either as carbon dioxide or as soot? Is it equal to millions of bags of charcoal? Tens of millions?

Get two children to unroll the number. The amount of carbon that goes into the atmosphere each year is the same as this number of bags of charcoal. Imagine the size of a mountain of that number of bags of charcoal! It is 5.7 billion tonnes.

NO RESPECT FOR GOD'S CREATION

Burning all this carbon causes pollution. The worst area of the world for pollution is the former Soviet Union and its satellite countries. In Poland, one third less sunlight reaches the ground because it is cut out by pollution. One Pole said,

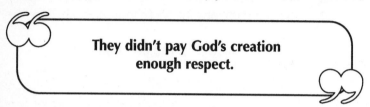

They didn't pay God's creation enough respect.

Is it a coincidence that in the Soviet Union for three quarters of a century the government claimed that God did not exist and tried to put an end to all religion?

Of course, it is not only "they" who do not pay God's creation enough respect. We are all guilty – including those of us who go to school in a car when we could walk!

But if it was people who said that God did not exist who made the biggest mistakes, perhaps it is those who listen to God who will best be able to help put things right.

✦ **A PRAYER**

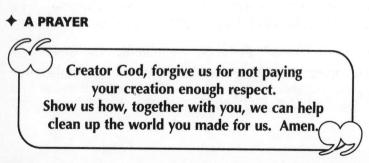

**Creator God, forgive us for not paying your creation enough respect.
Show us how, together with you, we can help clean up the world you made for us. Amen.**

POPULATION EXPLOSION

✦ THEME
A Christian approach to the problems caused by an exploding world population.

✦ YOU WILL NEED
- large sheets of paper with these figures written on them: 6,000,000,000 and 1,000,000,000+

✦ PRESENTATION
Tell children near the front that you are going to count and to point at them. As you point at each individual, he or she is to stand up.

Start counting and pointing at one-second intervals: "One baby, two babies, three babies, four babies ..." etc – up to thirty.

Each person standing represents a new baby who has actually just been born somewhere in the world.

One baby is born every second.

Bring the thirty children out to the front and say that they represent the 6 billion in the world now. Give one of the paper to hold with 6,000,000,000 written on it.

Separate ten of the thirty: these represent the children.

One third of the present world population is children.

They need food, housing, healthcare and schools.

Now separate six of the twenty 'adults'. These are the ones who can't find work in the developing countries, the poorer countries of the world. Of the remaining fourteen, some are too old to work and need care. The ones who have work must support all the others.

Bring out six more children to join the thirty at the front. This is the extra number of people there are going to be in the world in the next ten years, more than one billion of them. Give one of them the 1,000,000,000+ sheet.

Where are we going to find the food, the hospitals, the work, the schools for all these as well? It sounds like an impossible task, doesn't it.

Do you think anyone knows the answer?

Do you know what is probably the most famous verse in the Bible, John 3:16? It begins,

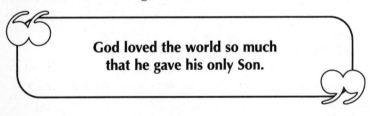

**God loved the world so much
that he gave his only Son.**

GOD KNOWS THE ANSWERS
Christians believe that God is the Creator of the world and that God loves the world and all the people in it. If he is clever enough to create the world, he is clever enough to know the answers. Because he loves us, but hasn't made us like robots, he wants us to listen to him for those answers.

Christians believe that whenever someone listens to God, the answers start to get worked out. It might be the voice of conscience inside us telling us not to be greedy or selfish.

It might be an interest or a skill that we have that, as we grow up, leads to a job God wants us to do.

It might be the feeling of excitement that some of us get when we discover new things. Maybe some of us here will discover new answers to some of the problems.

Conscience, interests, excitement – these are all ways God can speak to us and show us what to do.

The problems of feeding and caring for all these people in the world are vast. But God is even bigger. Christians believe that when we work with him, we can work it out. Every single one of us can be a part of God's answer.

✦ SOMETHING TO THINK ABOUT
Here are some thoughts from *Psalm 33*. They might be read out or written on OHP to think about while some music is played.

> **The Lord watches over those who obey him,**
> **those who trust in his constant love.**
> **He saves them from death,**
> **he keeps them alive in times of famine.**
>
> *Psalm 33:18-19*, Good News Bible.

✦ FOLLOW-UP

Work with a small group of children on presenting the whole of *Psalm 33* as a dramatic or choral reading. (Recommended version: International Children's Bible.)

This can be introduced by a recap of the figures above. The people of Israel faced problems of war and hunger that were as great to them as the present world problems are to us. This is a poem or song that shows how they faced those problems.

The last three verses and the first three encourage us not to get overwhelmed by thinking about problems, but to trust God and have a good sing!

DON'T GET CAUGHT!

HOOKED!

✦ THEME
The dangers of being 'hooked' by addictions, and how some people find freedom.

✦ YOU WILL NEED
- some real fishing tackle OR two canes and string with some suitable sweets tied on (eg. red liquorice 'bootlaces')
- two blindfolds

✦ PRESENTATION
You could talk seriously about fishing, or have a fun fishing contest between two pairs of children. One of each pair holds the cane (keeping the end well up in the air away from eyes) and the other is blindfolded and keeps his hands behind his back. He has to catch and eat the 'bait' off the end of the line. Quickest pair wins.

What do people get 'hooked' on?

Start with one or two examples; the children may be able to suggest others. Eg video games, scratch cards, food, drugs, alcohol, stealing. It can even be things like gossiping or telling tall stories.

What happens to people who get hooked on such things?

Talk about how hard it is to escape. The funny thing is, those who get hooked often start by thinking they are being really free! We probably all know someone who started smoking because they thought it looked 'big' and now would like to stop but can't.

THE BAIT THE DISCIPLES USED

Jesus told some of his first disciples that they were going to be 'fishers of men'. What sort of bait did they use to catch people? It was things like: the promise of eternal life; freedom from guilt; understanding what life is all about; being filled with the Spirit of God.

People who get 'caught' by this bait find something strange: they claim they are set free! Jesus actually said about himself, **"If the Son sets you free, you will be free indeed."** (*John 8:36*)

A man called Rick Toseland had been on drugs for five years. One night he got 'caught' at a Salvation Army meeting when he asked Jesus to take his addiction from him. The next morning he woke up free from the usual over-powering need for drugs. Rick said, "As far as I know, it is medically impossible to come off drugs overnight with no withdrawal symptoms, no medication. But with God, anything is possible."[1]

The best thing is to avoid the temptation of the bait in the first place. But if we do get hooked, let's remember that there are many people like Rick Toseland who tell us that there is a way to be set free – through Jesus.

✦ A PRAYER

Lord Jesus, help me to find real freedom, the freedom to be the person you made me to be. Help me to recognise temptations when they come, and give me the courage to say 'no'. Amen.

[1] Quoted in JESUS NOW! Magazine, Issue 1.

DOG SWORD-SWALLOWER

✦ THEME
The seriousness of stealing.

✦ YOU WILL NEED
- a Bible: *Proverbs 28:24*

✦ PRESENTATION
Talk about birthdays and birthday cakes. Have the children ever been tempted to have a bite of their birthday cake before it was cut at the party?

There was a dog with the rather strange name of Apple who lived in New York. His owner had made a birthday cake and left it sitting on a table. It was too much of a temptation for Apple. He tucked into the tasty cake, but he was in so much of a hurry to bolt it down that he managed to do a sword-swallowing act with the knife that was being used to cut it!

Fortunately for Apple, the knife went down handle first, or his greed could have been fatal. His owner discovered him with the blade sticking out of his mouth and was able to deliver him from his embarrassing predicament. How's that for being caught red-handed!

Do animals know the difference between right and wrong? They certainly know when their owners don't approve of what they do. Both dogs and cats seem to look guilty when caught stealing some food that is not theirs.

We humans do know that stealing is wrong. But sometimes we try to excuse ourselves by saying it was only something small.

Listen to what is says in the Bible:

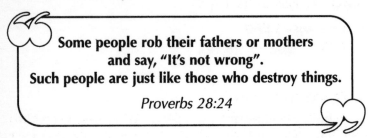

**Some people rob their fathers or mothers
and say, "It's not wrong".
Such people are just like those who destroy things.**

Proverbs 28:24

In other words, even taking something small at home without permission – a few coins, or cake or biscuits – is as bad as smashing things up. God knows what we are like. The small things we do wrong at home may develop into much bigger things.

Apple got caught in his crime when it went horribly wrong. We may get away with small things most of the time, but there may come a time when it goes horribly wrong. The best way not to get caught like Apple is not to start stealing in the first place.

✦ SOMETHING TO DO
Children could draw a picture of Apple doing his sword-swallowing act. Underneath they could write a prayer asking God to help them resist temptation.

BEASTLY BULLFROG

✦ THEME

A warning against being greedy.

✦ YOU WILL NEED

- a Bible: *Luke 12:15-21*

✦ PRESENTATION

Have you ever heard the story of Hungry Hagar the beastly bullfrog? Hagar was one of the residents at the Stratford-upon-Avon Butterfly and Jungle Safari centre.

One summer staff at the centre noticed that their butterflies were disappearing. Up to twenty of these beautiful and expensive creatures were vanishing every day. Many of them had been specially imported from all over the world.

At first they suspected an iguana, but he turned out to be a vegetarian. Then a watch was kept on a group of cockatoos. For weeks staff were scratching their heads, unable to find the culprit.

Finally one of them spotted Hagar tucking into one of his cousins, another bullfrog almost as big as himself. For dessert he sprang into the air and snapped up a butterfly in mid-flight.

Catching Hungry Hagar proved almost as difficult as unmasking him. Staff had to wait until the sleepiness of hibernation slowed him down. His punishment? – solitary confinement in a glass case.

"He had an insatiable appetite," said Mr Lamb, the manager. "He was very fat when we eventually caught him. Now we are feeding him on locusts, which are much cheaper."

A MAN WHO WAS GREEDY

Being greedy is very unpleasant. Jesus told a story about a kind of human Hagar. Only this man was greedy for money and things as well as food. Listen to what happened to him.

Read or tell the story of the Rich Fool in *Luke 12:15-21*.

✦ A REMINDER

Children could draw a picture of Hungry Hagar for display. Under it they could write Jesus' warning: "Be careful and guard against all kinds of greed."

AH... AH... AH... TISHOO!

✦ THEME
A thought for the season of colds and 'flu: protecting our minds as well as our bodies.

✦ YOU WILL NEED
• a clean handkerchief

✦ PRESENTATION
Start with the most dramatic sneeze you can manage.

What happens when we sneeze? We force air explosively from our lungs. The rushing air carries a spray of around 19,000 droplets as much as one metre. No wonder the old saying warned: Coughs and sneezes spread diseases; catch the germs in your handkerchiefses!

Also, when we sneeze we have to close our eyes. Researchers have discovered that it is impossible to keep your eyes open when you sneeze. This is a good job: the force of the sneeze is great enough to force your eyeballs out of their sockets!

Why do we sneeze? For protection. That tickle in the nose or throat might be a harmful foreign body that could be breathed or washed down into the lungs. The sneeze blasts it back out again. It is one of the many ways the body has of protecting itself.

Like many of the body's other defences, it is involuntary. That is to say, we can't make ourselves sneeze, and it is very hard to stop one that is coming. Sneezing is outside the conscious control of our minds.

ROUND AND ROUND IN OUR HEADS

But what about our minds? What happens when something possibly harmful gets into them – something frightening or nasty that we see on the television, for example? Once such a picture is in our minds, it can't be sneezed out again. We all know what it is like when something keeps going round and round in our heads and we can't stop it.

That is why we need to be careful about what we watch. It is why some programmes can only be shown after nine o'clock in the evening when children should be in bed. It is best not to let harmful things get into our minds in the first place. Sometimes friends or older children or even an adult might want us to watch a video that shows things that are wrong. **To protect ourselves we have to say 'no'.**

St Paul puts it more positively like this:

> **Continue to think about the things that are good and worthy of praise.**
>
> **Think about the things that are true and honourable and right and pure and beautiful and respected.**
>
> *Philippians 4:8*

That is good advice.

Some people like to play jokes with sneezing powder. Others might want you to look at a magazine or video they've got. Protect your mind. Just say no.

✦ A PRAYER

> God, we thank you for designing our
> bodies with lots of ways to protect themselves
> from harm.
>
> Make us aware when something we see or hear
> might be harmful to our minds.
> Give us the courage to say no.
>
> Amen.

GUIDELINES FOR GOOD COMMUNICATORS

ENJOY YOURSELF!

The blindfold fishing game in HOOKED! is great fun. In a different way, so is the story of Hungry Hagar in BEASTLY BULLFROG. Both create ripples of laughter.

Laughter is a great way of coming alongside children. It establishes common ground, is a beginning of friendship, and breaks down possible barriers.

When we enjoy presenting a talk to children, that in itself communicates a very positive message about the ideas and lifestyle we are advocating. After all, joy is a keynote of the Kingdom of God.

And there is no contradiction in having fun and presenting a serious message at the same time. Indeed, it models a very healthy and balanced approach to life. This is especially important when we are tackling issues of potentially harmful vices such as those in this section. Coming across as too serious – being seen as a kill-joy – can actually provoke in children the opposite reaction to that intended.

So relax and have fun. Enjoy yourself!

1 IN 14,000,000

✦ **THEME**

A graphic illustration of the chance of winning the lottery jackpot.

✦ **YOU WILL NEED**

- a stack of 10p coins and a marker pen; perhaps a mock giant cheque for £10million.

✦ **PRESENTATION**

You might start by asking for a show of hands: how many of the children's (or their friends') families buy lottery tickets each week? ... We are going to look at the chances of winning the jackpot.

Show children the 10p coins and mark one clearly on one face with the marker pen. Tell them that you are going to hide the marked coin somewhere in a stack of 10p's and you want them to imagine that if they choose the right coin, they will win the lottery jackpot.

(Show the giant cheque if you have made one.)

To get the odds right, we are going to need some more 10p pieces. The stack will reach the ceiling. Then we'll need a crane to keep building it as high as the Eiffel Tower. After that, it gets a bit difficult. We can perhaps get as high as Ben Nevis in Britain, over 4000 feet high, but we are still not there. A few more lorry-loads of coins and we'll reach as high as Mount Everest. After that, we'll have to use a plane to keep adding coins to the top of the stack. Up and up, as high as a jet airliner at 30,000 feet – but we are not even half-way there yet! We need to keep on adding 10p's until we get a stack over 26,000 metres high, or more than 26 kilometres.

Now we've got the stack finished, roll up, roll up! Anyone who wants to can pay £1 and choose just one 10p out of that pile 26 km high. If you choose the right one, you win the jackpot! Any takers?

Is picking the winning coin out of that pile a realistic dream? That is exactly the same chance as winning the jackpot with a £1 lottery ticket.

Wise King Solomon once said this:

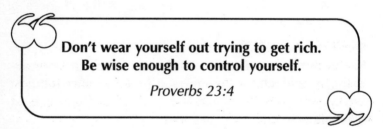

**Don't wear yourself out trying to get rich.
Be wise enough to control yourself.**

Proverbs 23:4

A person who spent large amounts of time and money trying to find the one right coin in a pile 26km high would surely wear themselves out for nothing. How much wiser to control ourselves and think through the best way to use our money.

✦ SOMETHING TO DO
Ask for suggestions of wiser ways to spend £1.

NOTE For four more talks on how Jesus viewed the use of money, see the section MONEY! MONEY! MONEY! in *52 IDEAS FOR JUNIOR CLASSROOM ASSEMBLIES* by Chris Chesterton and Pat Gutteridge (Monarch 1995).

IT COULD BE YOU (BY 20,000 AD)

Mathematics is not everyone's strong point, else the national lottery would hardly command the following it does. (But then, Camelot was ever the realm of impossible dreams.) Some children might find this presentation of salient figures gives pause for thought. (But perhaps that too is just wishful thinking?)

✦ THEME
The wise use of money.

✦ YOU WILL NEED
• two large pieces of paper with these figures on: £11,817 and -£5,070.

✦ PRESENTATION
Ask for two volunteers who would like to help in an experiment by spending a few thousand pounds over the next twenty years. We'll call them Jo and Chris. Stand one on either side of you.

Jo and Chris both get £5 a week pocket money. Jo spends around £3 of hers each week and gets her dad to buy her two Lottery tickets with the rest. She is hoping to win the jackpot and become a millionaire.

Chris also spends £3 a week, but would rather save the rest so he has it to use some day. He puts £2 a week into a Building Society.

Five years later they both have a bit more spending money – £10 a week. Jo decides to double her lottery tickets. Chris also doubles the amount he saves.

Another five years on and they are both out at work. Jo now spends £8 a week on lottery tickets, and Chris puts £8 a week into his savings account.

Finally, five years later, Jo can afford to spend £16 a week on lottery tickets in the hope of winning the big one, whilst Chris increases his savings to £16 a week.

Let's see how they are likely to be doing after 20 years.

Jo has spent £7,800 on lottery tickets. Has she won a million pounds? Almost certainly not. She has probably won smaller prizes totalling around £2,730. So overall she has lost £5,070. (Give 'Jo' the minus £5,070 sign.)

Chris has put the same amount, £7,800, into his savings account. With interest it now comes to over £11,800. (Give 'Chris' the £11,817 sign.[1]) As the wise King Solomon said,

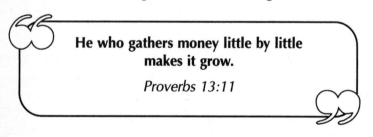

He who gathers money little by little makes it grow.

Proverbs 13:11

Minus £5,070 on one side, plus £11,817 on the other – Chris is almost £17,000 better off than Jo.

---

[1] This figure is based on a 6% interest rate.

What happens if Jo goes on buying lottery tickets in the hope of choosing the six right numbers?

If she spends at the rate she has done over the past 20 years, it will take her until the year 20,000 (yes, twenty thousand!) to have even a one in two chance of winning the jackpot. That's another 180 centuries. By that time she will have spent over £70 million on tickets.

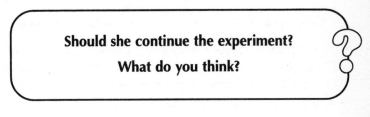

Should she continue the experiment?

What do you think?

WARNING SIGNS

THANK YOU, GOD, FOR PAIN!

✦ THEME
Pain is a valuable warning that something is wrong.

We live in a culture that views pain almost as an evil in itself, as bad as the things that cause the pain. The shocked response of children when one suggests that we should thank God for pain is most instructive.

✦ YOU WILL NEED
- a garden cane and a ruler; perhaps a copy of the *Beano*
- OR a hammer, nails and a piece of wood

✦ PRESENTATION
Make a show of swishing the cane around. Today's children have not met with this as an instrument of punishment (unlike some of us of the older generation!) but they will be familiar with the Beano's Bash Street school.

Swap the cane for a ruler (less dangerous) and get a volunteer to hit you across the hand with it. (It might need two or three attempts to get them to do more than tap you with it.) Shout 'Ow!' and make a fuss about how much it hurt. Then get the volunteer to sit down and say that you have a prayer to say this morning. Your prayer is:

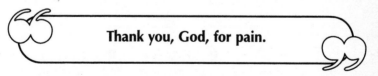

Thank you, God, for pain.

Alternative introduction. Do a bit of carpentry or hammer in a picture hook and pretend to hit your thumb with the hammer. Then go on to the prayer, as above.

AN ENCOUNTER WITH LEPROSY

Ask the children if they think you are crazy? (A frustrated Bash St. teacher, perhaps?) Why should we thank God for pain? A famous doctor gives us the answer.

As a boy, Paul Brand lived in India. His father was a doctor and a missionary. He vividly remembers the only time in his life he saw his father hesitate to help someone.

He was seven years old at the time. Three men came to the Brands' house one day for medical treatment. As they approached, Paul noticed a difference from the hundreds of others who came. Their skin was thick and mottled, their ears were swollen. They had blood-stained bandages around their feet. Closer still, Paul saw they had fingers missing, and one had no toes.

Paul's mother came out, and her face went pale. She told Paul to run and get his father and then to shut himself inside the house.

Full of curiosity, Paul slipped out of the house and found a hiding place where he could watch. He saw his father put on surgical gloves – this was most unusual. As he watched his father bathing and dressing the men's wounds, he realised that they were not wincing or crying out in pain.

> **This was Paul's first encounter with leprosy, the oldest recorded and most dreaded disease in the world.**

When he grew up, Paul became a doctor himself, and a world authority on leprosy. In his studies of leprosy patients in India he discovered that the disease is not like some fungus, eating away at fingers and noses, but that it simply attacks the nerve cells. Gradually the sufferer loses the sense of pain in parts of his body.

So he traps a finger and doesn't even notice. Or twists an ankle and continues to walk on it. Or his eyelids stop blinking away dust and dirt and he goes blind.

Pain is the body's alarm-system. It tells us that the dish we have just picked up is too hot and that we need to put it down quickly before we get burned. It is our first line of defence against harm.

None of us like pain – it would not be much good as an alarm-system if we did. But without it we would be in serious trouble. Perhaps you can join me now in my strange prayer:

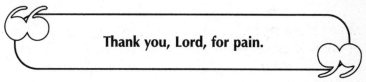

Thank you, Lord, for pain.

The story is taken from *FEARFULLY AND WONDERFULLY MADE* by Dr Paul Brand and Philip Yancey (Hodder and Stoughton, London, 1981) pp 35-37.

TSET GWILLEPS

✦ **THEME**
Misunderstanding God's rules for living.

✦ **YOU WILL NEED**
- a list of words for a backwards spelling test, eg honey, seven, milk, race, football, thumb, white, mouse, town, school
- a Bible: *Mark 3:1-6* and *2:27*

✦ **PRESENTATION**
Either ask for volunteers and give them words to be spelt backwards, eg honey – y-e-n-o-h, or you spell them backwards and ask for hands up, who can tell you the word.

Tell the story of Jesus and the man with the shrivelled hand in *Mark 3:1-6.* This is a story about people who had got things backwards.

If necessary, explain that the synagogue was the place where Jewish people went to worship God and listen to teaching, like a church or a mosque. The Sabbath is Saturday, the Jewish holy day. The Jews had very strict laws about not doing any work on the Sabbath. Many Jews keep similar laws today.

The religious leaders of the time had got things backwards. Jesus said,

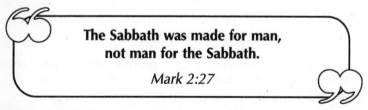

**The Sabbath was made for man,
not man for the Sabbath.**

Mark 2:27

In other words, God's rules for living are to help us live fuller, not more restricted, lives. In the Fourth Commandment, God told people 'to observe the Sabbath and keep it holy'. It is a day for resting from work and remembering how God created the world and himself rested on the seventh day. God did not intend it to be a burden on people in which keeping rules actually stopped them doing good.

> **Would Jesus tell us off for getting things backwards, like he told off the religious leaders then?**
>
> **Perhaps the way in which we have turned 'holy days' into 'holidays' when we just do what we like and not think about God at all makes Jesus sad.**
>
> **What do you think?**

✦ A PRAYER

Lord Jesus, you were angry at the religious leaders, but you also felt sorry for them because they were so stubborn and wrong. Help us to understand God's rules for living aright, and not to be stubborn. Amen.

GUIDELINES FOR GOOD COMMUNICATORS

SURPRISE THEM

I love the reaction you get in a group of children when you pray, "Thank you, God, for pain!"

Is this guy just mildly nutty or final proof of the failure of Care in the Community?

Surprise is a great way of getting genuine attention. It can range from the shock tactic of a loud noise or shout, to the gentler effect of producing of a strange object, or to unexpected actions or words as above. It often provokes laughter.

Surprise can raise a question in the minds of children so that they keep listening until they get an answer. It can persuade them to see things from a fresh viewpoint. It helps make a message memorable.

Jesus used shock and surprise in his teaching. Telling people to behave like a hated Samaritan is one example; an employer paying his workers as much for one hour as for a whole day is another.

The day Jesus arrived in Jericho on his final journey to Jerusalem was a day of surprises. Here was a man being talked about as the promised Messiah choosing to stay with that despised collaborator with Romans, Zacchaeus! The message Jesus gave through that choice was very much the same as the surprising conclusion of BUZZ OFF!

LIZARD MUESLI

✦ THEME
Watching what we say.

✦ YOU WILL NEED
- a bowl of cereal, a spoon, and a prune or large raisin
- a Bible: *Mark 7:14-23*. (This passage could be split into sections and given to a couple of children to prepare.)

✦ PRESENTATION
Apologise for being late with your breakfast and start tucking into a bowl of cereal. Hold up a spoon with a large raisin or prune in it and tell this story about a teacher from Bristol.

He was eating his breakfast muesli when he found what he thought was a dried prune. Fortunately, he examined it carefully before putting it into his mouth. He discovered that it was a small, dried up lizard! This tree lizard, a black iguanid, had got itself mistaken for a large Californian raisin. (Eat your prune and declare it to be 'very tasty'.)

The makers and suppliers of that brand of muesli were fined £3,500 each for failing to take enough care about their product. Foreign bodies in food are rare, but some of those that do happen quite turn your stomach over.

Ask for a show of hands – who likes pizza? ... Would they have liked the variety served up by one Dutch take-away? Its extra special, mouth-watering topping was ... horse manure!

Then there were the boxes of porridge oats sold by a super-market in East London. They were found to contain more than 1000 beetles and 5000 grubs, all of them alive.

Not forgetting the well-known brand chocolate slice with the extra, rather chewy ingredient – a cigarette end.

Tales such as that make us feel quite queasy. What goes into our mouths can be pretty worrying, But what comes out of our mouths can be just as bad. (And we are not talking about being sick after hearing the tales above.)

Have children read the prepared Bible passage: *Mark 7:14-23.*

Jesus is saying that we should be a lot more worried about the words that come out of our mouths than the food that goes into them. What would happen if we got a £3,500 fine today each time we said something bad about someone else or had a nasty thought?

Most of us would be very heavily in debt by the end of the day!

✦ A PRAYER

Father God, help us to keep nasty things out of our minds, and, most especially, to keep a guard over our mouths so that nasty and hurtful words do not come out of them. Amen.

BUZZZZ OFF!

✦ THEME
A lesson from nature about the dangers of judging others.

✦ YOU WILL NEED
- a picture of a wasp. Find one in a nature book or copy these onto OHP acetate or get some children to draw their own versions.

✦ PRESENTATION
Find out how many people have been stung by a wasp this year? ... Who's allergic to wasp stings? ... Who's frightened of wasps? ... Who doesn't mind them buzzing around?

Did you know that there are thousands of different kinds of wasp? The smallest are microscopic, and the largest queen is 4cm long with an 8cm wingspan. Fortunately she lives in the Himalayas so there is not too much chance of meeting her!

> **Try a vote. If we could get rid of all wasps from the earth, who would vote for that? ...**

Anybody in favour of keeping wasps? ... Why? ... Can anyone think of any good that wasps might do?

In fact, wasps play a vital ecological role. One of the jobs they do is to pollinate flowers, like bees. They are not quite so important in the ecosystem as bees, but they still do a lot of essential work.

Take fig trees, for example. In the world's rainforests figs are the most important source of food for fruit-eating animals. Each of the many different species of fig has its own type of wasp to pollinate it. The fig and the wasp are entirely dependent on each other. Without the wasps the figs would not be pollinated and no fruit would grow. Without the fruit countless animals would die. A large part of the rainforest ecosystem would collapse.

Perhaps even more important is the way they control the numbers of other insect pests. The painful sting that we know is a development of a paralysing poison that many wasps use. The wasp attacks a spider, a caterpillar or a grub and paralyzes it. Then she takes it to a nest she has made – perhaps a hole in wood or soil, or one made out of mud – and she lays an egg on or in it. When the wasp larva hatches out it feeds on the paralyzed insect or spider.

It sounds horrible! But if the wasps weren't quietly getting on feeding their larvae in this way, populations of other pests might explode and upset their ecosystem. People might lose crops or have to use chemical pesticides. The sawfly, a serious pest in North America that was destroying spruce trees, was controlled by introducing wasps.

It's a good job we were not able to really vote wasps out of existence. Just think: we would have killed millions of other animals in the rainforests and wrecked whole ecosystems all over the world!

> Things are rarely as simple as they seem. Perhaps that's why Jesus warned us not to judge each other. Somebody might be a real pest, but there are certainly all kinds of good things about them that we aren't even aware of. Perhaps we should think of the wasp before telling them to buzz off!

✦ **A PRAYER**

> Great Creator God, you designed the world
> and all the plants and animals in it.
> You did a good job. You made all the people, too.
> When I am tempted to judge somebody because
> I don't like something about them, remind me
> of the wasp. Amen.

SUPER INJUSTICE

✦ **THEME**
Injustice

✦ **YOU WILL NEED**
• a picture, comic or video of Superman

✦ **PRESENTATION**
Ask children to raise their hands if they have heard of Joe Shuster. (If anyone does, ask who they think he is.) Then ask who has heard of Superman. Display a Superman comic or video if you have one. Joe Shuster was the artist who created Superman.

While still at school, aged seventeen, Shuster teamed up with another student, Jerry Siegel. Siegel was the writer, with an especial liking for science fiction. Together they began producing comic strips for their school newspaper. They also sent off examples to national newspapers, but all of them were rejected.

It was in 1936 that Siegel and Shuster got their first real break, with two series in a comic called 'More Fun'. Two years later, Superman made his first appearance in 'Action Comics No 1'. If you had a mint copy of that in good condition today it would be worth more than £40,000!

Joe Shuster died in 1992. As Superman had starred in at least forty-four comic book series, plus radio, T.V., and film series, and four of the world's biggest money-making movies, Joe Shuster should have died a very rich man. But he wasn't.

UNFAIR TREATMENT

For many years he had been almost penniless. His eyesight had started failing and he had had to retire early. For many years he was supported by his wife Joanna, the original model for Lois Lane. He and Jerry Siegel had fought in the courts for a share in the Superman profits for nearly forty years but had got nowhere.

It was only when Warner Brothers was launching the first Superman movie that they agreed to give $20,000 a year each to Siegel and Shuster. At less than £15,000 a year it was hardly over-generous, and Joe did not live many more years to enjoy it.

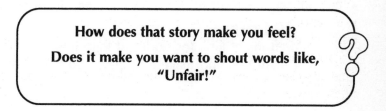

How does that story make you feel?

Does it make you want to shout words like, "Unfair!"

Superman was always fighting for justice – that is, treating people right, fairly – yet his creators were treated most unfairly.

Unfair treatment – injustice – is all around us. Sometimes it is much worse than the example we have just heard. (You could mention an example from current news.) Sometimes we are part of it ourselves, perhaps without realizing it, as when people in Third World countries are treated little better than slaves to produce food we eat or clothes we wear.

We may not have super powers, but we ought all to be involved in the fight against injustice. There are some famous words from the Bible we could think about or use as a prayer. This was spoken by the prophet Amos, a man who hated injustice:

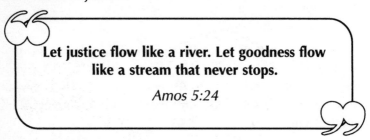

Let justice flow like a river. Let goodness flow like a stream that never stops.

Amos 5:24

✦ SOMETHING TO DO
Older children might look for stories of injustice in newspapers, cut them out, and make a display. Add the words from Amos 5:24.

TREASURES OF DARKNESS 1

✦ THEME
Treasure from the natural world tells us about a generous God.

✦ YOU WILL NEED
- a number of items made (or partly made) from plastics eg yoghurt pot, cola bottle, ball-pen, radio or cassette-player, piece of polystyrene, article of clothing made of nylon, etc.

✦ PRESENTATION
Show your collection and ask the children to think how many other things they will use today made of some kind of plastic.

> **Does anyone know where all this plastic comes from?**

Does it grow on trees?

Are there genetically mutated cows that have plastic skins instead of leather?

Are there armies of children in Asia working sixteen hours a day pulling wings off flies to make polythene bags?

The answer is: oil, crude oil – or petroleum, to give it its proper name. It's that black stuff we get on us on the beach during the summer holidays because a tanker of crude oil has had a spillage somewhere.

Petroleum was known in the ancient world because there are places where the sticky, tarry, crude oil seeps out on the surface. They used it to caulk ships and even sometimes to build roads. Those uses were valuable enough, but they could not have dreamed of the riches hidden away inside that sticky black stuff.

Its first main use in the modern world came when it was refined to produce oil to be burned in lamps and replace oil from whales. So one thing it has done is to help save the whale! The first oil well was drilled in the United States in 1859.

IMAGINE A WORLD WITHOUT PLASTICS
Today oil is the major source of power in the world, driving virtually all our cars, lorries and planes. And it is not only plastics that are made from it, but solvents, paints, asphalt, fibres for clothes, soap, cleansing agents, explosives, fertilizers, and even medicines. Could we imagine a world now without them?

Centuries ago the prophet Isaiah spoke this message from God to Cyrus, king of Persia:

> **I will give you the treasures of darkness, riches stored in secret places, so that you may know that I am the Lord, the God of Israel, who summons you by name.**
>
> *Isaiah 45:3,* New International Version

When we look at the use we make of the crude oil that comes from deep under the earth or under the North Sea, it seems as if God has said that to the whole human race. He has given us treasures of darkness, riches stored in secret places.

✦ **A PRAYER**

Thank you for ball-pens and cola bottles,
cassettes and CD's, trainers and TV sets.
Thank you for the men and women who
have discovered the 'treasures of darkness'
and given us so much to use and enjoy
every single day.

Amen.

TREASURES OF DARKNESS 2

✦ THEME
Discovering the treasures inside us.

✦ YOU WILL NEED
- ask a group of children aged eight or older to make a list of things they can do now which they could not do when they started school. If they are able to identify skills rather than knowledge, so much the better.

✦ PRESENTATION
Recap on the previous talk about crude oil and what can be made from it.

Through accident or research, people are constantly discovering new resources and riches hidden not just in oil but in countless other things in the natural world around us. New ways of treating and changing and refining substances are being discovered to provide even more materials.

But you don't have to be a scientist to discover riches hidden in secret places. Every one of us has hidden skills, gifts and understanding.

Ask the group to come and talk about some of the skills they have discovered since they started going to school.

> **Have they enjoyed discovering these things? ...**
>
> **Have they 'refined' them – that is, improved them? ...**
>
> **Are they proud of their achievements? ...**

A big part of the excitement of life is discovering and refining the resources buried inside ourselves. Going to school is one part of that process of discovery and refining.

When we look at the world around us, and then look at ourselves, it is as if the whole world is a treasure house. One of the main purposes and joys of life is to discover that treasure, bring it into the light, and use it. And what did the prophet Isaiah say the reason was for all this?

> **So that you may know that I am the Lord, the God of Israel, who summons you by name.**
>
> *Isaiah 45:3*

✦ A DIFFERENT KIND OF PRAYER

We can give a clap to the people who talked about their discoveries of things they had learnt. As we clap them, we can also clap God who created us with those resources inside us waiting to be discovered.

GUIDELINES FOR GOOD COMMUNICATORS

THE 'YUK!' FACTOR

You don't need to be unusually squeamish to get a shiver from the thought of the eccentric food additives in LIZARD MUESLI or the benign attentions of the maggots in CREEPY-CRAWLY.

The 'Yuk!' factor in a talk plays much the same part as laughter or surprise. It gains attention, creates questions, and ensures memorability. You can be sure that horse-dung pizza and flesh-munching maggots are going to get talked about in the playground and over the take-away.

As recorded in John 6, Jesus so offended people with his words about eating his flesh and drinking his blood that it drove many of them away. Yet there can be no doubt that this teaching lodged in their minds.

The 'Yuk!' factor is one to be used sparingly, but is a helpful addition to any communicator's toolbag.

BEAUTY ON THE INSIDE

✦ THEME
A Spring-time analogy from nature and a Greek myth shows that our inner gifts are more important than outward appearance.

✦ YOU WILL NEED
- a bowl or a bunch of daffodils (or, out of season, a daffodil bulb);
- perhaps a mirror.

✦ PRESENTATION

> **Which is more important: how we look on the outside, or what kind of person we are?**

Perhaps a bunch of daffodils can teach us something. They certainly look pretty and cheer us up after the dreary days of winter. But scientists have recently discovered something inside the dull-looking daffodil bulb that could do certain people even more good than admiring the flowers.

Daffodils belong to the narcissus family of plants – some of the daffodil-type flowers you can grow or buy in the shops are called narcissi. There is an old Greek myth about these flowers and their beauty.

There was once a young man named Narcissus. He was extremely handsome, but his mother had been told when he was a baby that he would only live a long life provided he never looked at his own face in a mirror.

A nymph called Echo fell in love with Narcissus, but he rejected her. The gods were angry and decided to punish him. One day Narcissus sat down beside a pool of still, clear water. Looking into it, he saw for the first time the reflection of his own face. Never having seen himself in a mirror, Narcissus was so struck by the beauty of the face looking back at him from the water that he fell in love with it.

Of course, the face only existed while he remained gazing into the water. Whenever Narcissus moved away he lost sight of it. He was so much in love with his own reflection that he stayed on the bank of the pool until he pined away and died. On that very spot, a flower grew. It was named after him: a narcissus.

Even today, people who spend a long time admiring themselves in a mirror are called narcissistic.

INSIDE THE UGLY BULB

The daffodil bulb is quite ugly compared to the flower. It even has an unpleasant means of self-defence. To stop animals eating it, it contains a chemical that makes them feel sick. It doesn't sound as if this could be any use to anybody except the plant itself. But scientists have found that this chemical might help people who suffer from Alzheimer's disease.

Alzheimer's is a very unpleasant disease of the brain. People who suffer from it lose their memory and have difficulty speaking, even though they may not be very old. It is as hard for their families as for the person who has it. There is still no cure for Alzheimer's, and little doctors can do to help the people who get it. If the scientists are right, and the daffodil-bulb extract really does slow down the disease, many people will be extremely grateful.

So some of the fields in Lincolnshire are now growing beautiful flowers above the ground and and medicine under the ground.

A SPECIAL WAY TO HELP OTHERS

It is not wrong to be proud of the way we look – unless we get like Narcissus and spend too long admiring ourselves in the mirror! But like the daffodil bulb, there is something far more important hidden away inside every one of us – some special way of being able to help others.

Do you know what special way you have of being able to help others?

Maybe it is something you do, or the way you talk to people, or how you feel about things and show that.

The Bible puts it like this:

People look at the outside of a person, but the Lord looks at the heart.

1 Samuel 16:7

It is in 'the heart' – our innermost selves – that lies the desire and special way each one of us has of being able to help other people.

✦ A PRAYER
In a moment of quiet, each person could ask God to 'grow' that special way of being able to help others and to really use it.

CREEPY-CRAWLY OR DOCTOR'S FRIEND!

Here's a talk that rates really high for 'Yuk!' factor. You can guarantee it will get talked about at home.

✦ THEME
An enemy turns out to be a friend.

✦ YOU WILL NEED
• If you know a fisherman who will supply you with a few maggots, so much the better. No other preparation is needed – apart from practising a ghoulish horror-movie voice for maximum effect.

✦ PRESENTATION
Who has seen a fisherman's tin full of wriggling maggots? ... Or even a dead bird or animal covered with the repulsive white creatures gorging themselves on the rotting flesh until only the skeleton remains?

Now imagine them crawling over your bare skin! It's the stuff nightmares are made of.

Yet one day you might go to hospital with an injury and find the doctor saying,

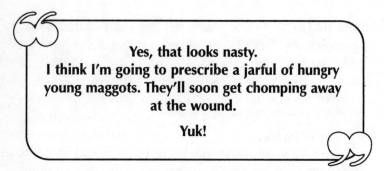

**Yes, that looks nasty.
I think I'm going to prescribe a jarful of hungry
young maggots. They'll soon get chomping away
at the wound.**

Yuk!

No, this isn't an April Fool or a scene from a horror film. It is a very effective way of helping a nasty wound to heal up quickly and to fight infection. It is already being used at some hospitals in Britain and other parts of the world.

This is why. Up to the 1930's, if you were injured in an accident or a battle, there was a serious risk that the wound would become infected. Often the only answer was amputation, otherwise the infection would spread though the body and kill you. Then penicillin was discovered, and other antibiotics followed. We have all grown up in a world where an injection or a week's medicine does the trick and fear of serious infection has almost disappeared.

**Now, though, some bacteria are becoming
increasingly resistant to antibiotics.**

Despite drugs and dressings, that wound may not heal up. So doctors are rediscovering a method of treating wounds that was used before antibiotics, especially in the United States.

The maggots are bred from the eggs of a kind of fly, the greenbottle. They are sterilised so that they don't carry infections. Depending on how large the wound is, from half-a-dozen up to a few hundred maggots are placed in it under a special dressing. The patient does not feel anything. The maggots get to work eating dead and diseased tissue in the wound. Usually they are removed after three days. Doctors find that infections disappear and the wound heals quickly.

> **One doctor reckons that perhaps 2,000 patients each week around Britain could be suitable for treatment by maggots.**

It may sound revolting, but when you think about it, it is a natural way of promoting healing. Maggots are one of nature's environmental clean-up specialists.

Isn't it strange? We don't like flies such as the greenbottle because they spread disease – and they do. That is why it is important to keep food covered and not let flies land on it. Yet the larval form of the greenbottle, the maggot, is one of nature's ways of fighting disease. A creature that seems at first sight to be an enemy turns out to be a very valuable friend.

✦ A PRAYER
Creator God, you made this world with so many strange and wonderful things in it. Help us to look beyond our first reactions and discover new friends in unexpected places. Amen.

HIDDEN VALUE

✦ **THEME**
The unseen treasure of the kingdom of heaven.

✦ **YOU WILL NEED**
- some saffron – if you can afford it!
- a flower to show stamens
- perhaps a crocus bulb
- a Bible: *Matthew 13:44*

✦ **PRESENTATION**
Imagine it is spring-time and the crocuses are in bloom. Imagine me showing you a field full of white and purple crocuses and saying, "I'll give you these flowers if you give me everything you own. Your bike, your Saturn or Playstation, your Walkman, everything." How many of you would do that swap?

If I tell you that there is treasure in that field, would that help you make up your mind? I might tell you that you are staring right at the treasure, and yet you probably can't see it! If I say that it is worth three times as much as gold, would you believe me?

If I tell you that the treasure that you are staring at is the fluffy yellow bits in the middle of the crocus flower, the stamens (show these on a flower) you will probably think I am a raving nutcase!

But it is true. Crocus stamens are picked, dried and sold as saffron, the most expensive spice in the world. Ten strands – ten of these dried stamens – cost nearly £3 in the shops. That works out at over £4000 for 100g.

Saffron has been known and used for thousands of years. King Solomon mentioned it in the Bible. Buddhist monks use it to dye their robes golden yellow. Oriental cooks use it to colour and flavour rice and other dishes.

The Romans are said to have slept on saffron-pillows to cure hangovers. At around £10,000 at today's prices that is a highly expensive remedy for a night's over-indulgence!

A DIFFERENT SORT OF TREASURE
Jesus once told a story about a different sort of treasure in a field. Here is his story:

> The kingdom of heaven is like a treasure hidden in a field. One day a man found the treasure, and then he hid it in the field again.
>
> The man was very happy to find the treasure. He went and sold everything that he owned to buy that field.
>
> *Matthew 13:44*

What is Jesus telling us in this story?

What is so valuable that it is worth selling everything else for?

Why was the man so happy to find it?

Jesus is saying that there is a way of living that is better than any other way. That way of living is life in what he calls 'the kingdom of heaven' or 'the kingdom of God'. In other places he tells us a lot more about what it means to live that kind of life.

Life in God's kingdom is so much better than any other way of living that, like the treasure in the field, it is worth giving up everything else for. That does not mean that God actually usually asks people to give up everything and go and be a monk or a nun. But he might ask us to give up something which is getting in the way of living life in the best way possible.

You would not have given me all that you own as a swap for a field of crocuses. That is because you did not realise how much they are worth. The treasure was there to see, but you did not recognize it.

The kingdom of heaven is there to see, but many people do not recognize it. It is only when they discover its true value that they realise it is worth giving anything in order to be able to live life like that.

Who's going to plant crocuses in their garden for next spring?

✦ A PRAYER
If there is treasure to be found, I don't want to miss out on it! Lord God, give me eyes to see the real treasure and the courage to give up anything that is stopping me finding it. Amen.

HIDDEN HARVEST

✦ **THEME**
More of nature's treasure-trove.

✦ **YOU WILL NEED**
• if possible, collect a few wild fungi – most gardens or a stroll in the local wood should supply some specimens
• try leaving some bread or fruit out a week or two in advance to get a nice crop of mould
• at the very least, buy some mushrooms

✦ **PRESENTATION**
Show the children whatever examples of fungi you have. These are just a few of the thousands of fungi in the world. Some we can eat, whilst others are deadly poisonous. NEVER eat a wild mushroom without it being first identified by an expert. In France, people take them along to their local chemist's shop for identification!

Some mushrooms or toadstools can have strange effects. There is one called the common ink-cap which often grows in gardens, especially at the base of trees. People who know what they are looking for can eat the ink-cap perfectly safely. But if they drink a glass of beer or wine in the next few days they start to feel sick and sweat a lot and get really bad pins and needles!

If one species of mushroom contains a substance that has that sort of effect, what other good or harmful chemicals might be lurking in fungi?

Who knows what penicillin is and what it is used for? ...

Where does penicillin come from? ...

It comes from the common blue or green mould which grows on rotten food. Penicillin made from mouldy melons saved countless lives at the end of World War II and afterwards. Some of us here might never have been born if our grandparents lives hadn't been saved by penicillin!

CHINESE MUSHROOM HELPS HAY-FEVER

Who likes Chinese food? ... There is a type of mushroom called the Shitake mushroom which is often used in Chinese and Japanese cooking. It has been found to be helpful in treating stomach cancers. It also contains an anti-histamine and so can help relieve the symptoms of hay-fever.

Researchers are looking at more than 200 substances in fungi which have been found to have an effect on cancers. Lots of work remains to be done for any of these to be accepted as reliable medicines without harmful side-effects, but it shows what an extraordinary harvest there is hidden inside humble mushrooms, toadstools and moulds.

An Jewish song-writer once looked at the natural world and was astounded at all that God had provided in it. He wrote:

> **O Lord, what a variety you have made!**
> **And in wisdom you have made them all!**
> **The earth is full of your riches.**
>
> *Psalm 104:24, The Living Bible*

That long-ago song-writer could never have imagined the skills and techniques modern scientists have for bringing to light the hidden harvest in fungi and plants. But he had grasped the essential truth: in his wisdom God created a world with a bewildering variety of riches waiting to be discovered.

✦ A PRAYER

Father God, perhaps one day my life might be saved by a medicine made from a fungus. Thank you for the riches that you have stored away for us in this wonderful world. Amen.

A NUTTY QUESTION

This is the first of two talks featuring the humble, but surprising, peanut.

✦ **THEME**
What can come out of a simple question.

✦ **YOU WILL NEED**
• a packet of peanuts or a good American peanut-butter and jelly (jam) sandwich

✦ **PRESENTATION**
Feed some children with peanuts or the peanut-butter and jelly sandwich. *(NB – check they are not allergic to nuts.)* Tell them they are going to learn some surprising things about peanuts.

Take one child born as a slave, one peanut plant, and one silly question, and you get ... millions of people's lives improved! How come?

The child was George Washington Carver, the son of a slave woman in the southern United States of

America. The peanut plant and the silly question came later. Carver was born in 1860, and orphaned during the American Civil War. He was interested in the natural world around him, and he also took up drawing, singing, and playing the organ. As a teenager and a young man, he supported himself with a variety of jobs – cook, laundryman, farm worker – while attending different schools and colleges to get an education. By the time he was in his thirties, he had gained a master of science degree.

In later years, he used to tell this story about what happened to him during this period of his life.

THE RIGHT SIZED QUESTION
One day while walking out in a field he said to God,

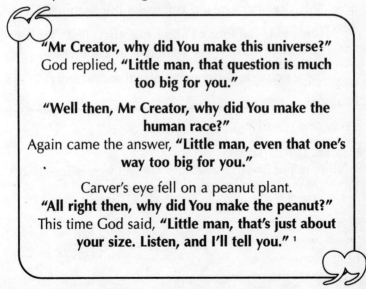

"Mr Creator, why did You make this universe?"
God replied, **"Little man, that question is much too big for you."**

"Well then, Mr Creator, why did You make the human race?"
Again came the answer, **"Little man, even that one's way too big for you."**

Carver's eye fell on a peanut plant.
"All right then, why did You make the peanut?"
This time God said, **"Little man, that's just about your size. Listen, and I'll tell you."** [1]

And George Washington Carver did listen. It may have sounded like a silly question, but the answer was far from silly. He got a job as the head of the department of agriculture at the Tuskegee Institute in Alabama. Working in his lab., Carver developed some 300 products made from peanuts, things as different and surprising as: cheese, milk, coffee, flour, ink, dyes, plastics, soap, floor-coverings, medicinal oils, and cosmetics. He often referred to God as his co-worker in the laboratory. With the agricultural training they received from him, black people whose parents had been slaves became skilled farmers. The whole economy of the Southern States of America was improved through the peanut industry.

> **"Mr Creator, why did You make the peanut?"**
>
> **How many millions of other questions like that are there waiting for someone to ask them?**
>
> **Have you asked any nutty questions recently?**

✦ SOMETHING TO DO

Children might like to think up some nutty questions to ask and share them the next time you meet.

[1] David Seamands, *Living With Your Dreams* (Scripture Press) p.178.

EAT A PEANUT AND THANK GOD!

✦ **THEME**
Finding hope in bad times.

✦ **YOU WILL NEED**
- some peanuts in their shells; a packet of roasted peanuts.

✦ **PRESENTATION**

If you want a nutritious snack, you can hardly do better than a packet of peanuts. They contain more protein, minerals and vitamins than liver, more fat than full-cream, and more energy than sugar. They are also just the snack to eat when you are feeling miserable because something has gone wrong – as we will discover in a moment.

Peanuts are not nuts at all. In fact, the 'pea' part of their name is more accurate. They grow in a most strange fashion. After the flowers on the small peanut bush fade, a stalk (called a peg) grows down from the base of each one and pushes right into the ground. As much as 10 cm under the surface, a pod starts to develop at the tip of the peg – the familiar peanut shell – and the seeds inside start to swell. To harvest the peanuts, the whole plant is pulled out of the ground and left to dry in the sun. (Show peanuts in their shells.)

There is an odd story about peanuts from the town of Enterprise in Alabama, America, centre of a peanut growing region. In the middle of the town is a unique monument built in the shape of a beetle. It is probably the only statue erected in the honour of a bug in the world! This area used to grow cotton, but in 1915 the crop was almost destroyed by a small beetle, the Mexican boll weevil. 60% of that year's cotton was lost. The desperate farmers turned to other crops, and were surprised at how much they earned growing peanuts. In 1917 they grew more peanuts than any other county in the nation. They were so grateful that in 1919 they erected the beetle statue. Written on it are these words:

In profound appreciation of the boll weevil,
And what it has done as the herald of prosperity.

In 1915 the farmers were cursing the beetle that was ruining them. Four years later they erected a monument in its praise! It reminds us of an old saying that sounds rather past its sell-by date, but which has a certain truth: Every cloud has a silver lining. What seems at the time to be a disaster may push us into thinking afresh about what we are doing, trying out something new, deciding what is important. The farmers of Enterprise discovered that they earned more money growing peanuts than cotton, and improved the soil as a bonus.

HELPING SPREAD THE GOOD NEWS

This is a truth that Christians have long known. For example, there is a story in the Bible about how Paul was taken to Rome as a prisoner to be judged by the Emperor. When he got there, he was allowed to live by himself, but chained to a Roman guard twenty-four hours a day. That sounds pretty terrible.

But Paul saw the good side of this. In one of his letters he wrote:

> **Brothers, I want you to know that what has happened to me has helped to spread the Good News. I am in prison because I am a believer in Christ. All the palace guards and everyone else knows this.**
>
> *Philippians 1:12-13*

Because different soldiers had spells on duty chained to Paul, they didn't have much choice but to listen to him. The whole of Caesar's crack troops, the palace guard, got to hear the message about Jesus! Paul was very pleased about that. Again and again in his letters as a prisoner he told people to be thankful.

So next time things go wrong, and you are feeling really low, why not buy a packet of peanuts? And while you're munching them, try Paul's recipe for happiness: thank God, and ask him to show you the silver lining in your cloud!

The boll weevil monument story is on p.170 of David Seamands, *Living With Your Dreams* (Scripture Press).

HIDDEN TREASURE

✦ THEME
The value of the Bible and the peace it promises.

✦ YOU WILL NEED
- an old, black Bible and a newer one with a red or colourful cover

✦ PRESENTATION
What would you do if you suddenly discovered you owned treasure worth nearly £400 million? ... This actually happened to a man in India a few years ago – but eighteen months later he hadn't spent a penny of it! In fact, Mr Vidyaraj was still living in an old house that he rented for £3.50 a month. All the money he had was the few pounds that his son in America sent him each month.

Mr Vidyaraj's treasure was precious stones: three of the biggest rubies in the world (the largest weighs 495 grams!) and the largest known double-star sapphire. They had been in his family for centuries, but they were so black with soot that no-one knew what they were. "They just looked like odd-shaped lumps of coal," he said.

One day he got to thinking about them and sent his family off to the cinema. When he cleaned them, he discovered what they were. It took some hard work with hot water and an old toothbrush before red and blue specks started to appear through the grime.

TREASURE ON A SHELF
Do you think you might have a treasure like that at home?

Sounds unlikely, doesn't it, just a nice daydream. But how about one of these? (Show black Bible). Perhaps you have one of these sitting on a shelf; maybe it has even been handed down in your family. It might never have occurred to you that there could be something very precious under the black cover.

Of course, it does help if the outside looks a bit more attractive. (Show coloured Bible). And it helps a lot if you can understand the language inside. Some people have thought that what this book contains was so valuable that they gave their lives translating it into their own everyday language.

Mr Vidyaraj was not too sure about selling his jewels. "I do have the urge for money," he said. "But I would be haunted by so many people – relatives, friends, the taxman, thieves – that my peace of mind would be lost."

> The funny thing is, that's part of the treasure the Bible promises: peace of mind. A lot of grown-ups would give anything for that.

£400 million or peace of mind? What a choice! But then, most of us don't have that choice. We don't have any odd-shaped pieces of coal sitting on a shelf. Lots of us do have Bibles, though ...

✦ SOMETHING TO DO
Children could use a computer Bible programme (or an old-fashioned concordance!) to find what Jesus said about peace. They could choose something to print out.

WISDOM - WORTH MORE THAN GOLD!

✦ THEME
Wisdom is the real treasure worth seeking for.

✦ YOU WILL NEED
- make a model of an Egyptian 'diadem' or coronet from card as in the drawing or copy the picture onto OHP acetate or paper.
- a Bible: *Proverbs 2:1-5*

✦ PRESENTATION
Get a volunteer to wear the diadem and introduce her as Queen Mentuhotep, the Great Royal Wife of an Egyptian king.[1]

Queen Mentuhotep lived in the town of Thebes (modern Luxor) some 3,500 years ago. This was roughly a century before Moses led the Israelites out of slavery in Egypt.

When she died, her body was mummified. This gold and silver diadem with two cobra's heads was placed on her bandaged head. She was buried in a tomb near the famous Valley of the Kings.

After that, there are only long centuries of darkness and mystery – until 1995, when two brothers decided to sell some bits and pieces that had belonged to their grandparents. By chance, an expert on ancient Egypt saw the coronet in the sale rooms. He recognised it as being like the only other one known to exist, which is in a museum in The Netherlands.

The brothers were astonished. They knew their grandparents were art historians, but had not realised that the blackened metal band was anything special. All though their childhood, a priceless gold and silver treasure had been sitting in a cabinet in their living room. They had given it no more thought than if it had been a souvenir mug from Blackpool!

Who likes watching one of the Antiques shows on TV? Probably most of us have dreamed of finding a treasure like this.

THE KING'S TREASURE
Another royal personnage – a king this time, not a queen – was very strong on the idea that treasure was there waiting for anyone who was prepared to really look for it. This king's name was Solomon. King Solomon had gold and silver in plenty, but he knew that there was something even more valuable. This was the advice he gave to young people:

> My child, believe what I say.
> And remember what I command you.
> Listen to wisdom.
> Try with all your heart to gain understanding.
> Cry out for wisdom.
> Beg for understanding.
> Search for it as you would for silver.
> Hunt for it like hidden treasure.
> Then you will understand what it means to respect the Lord.
> Then you will begin to know God.
>
> *Proverbs 2:1-5*

Wisdom? Understanding? Respecting the Lord? Knowing God? Some people would say, "Huh! Those are just some blackened old relics that might have interested my grandparents but aren't much use to me!"

There might only be a handful of people who thought it was worth following King Solomon's advice. Just a few who want to search for wisdom as they would for silver, or hunt for understanding like hidden treasure. They could be the ones who discover the real treasure.

✦ A PRAYER

Here is part of a prayer of King Solomon when he was young and God spoke to him in a dream. He realised how hard it was going to be to rule his people well. Anyone who wants to seek 'the king's treasure' can echo this prayer.

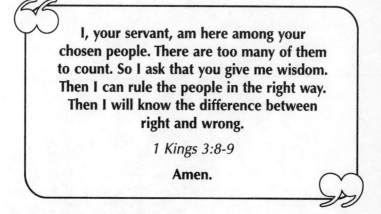

I, your servant, am here among your chosen people. There are too many of them to count. So I ask that you give me wisdom. Then I can rule the people in the right way. Then I will know the difference between right and wrong.

1 Kings 3:8-9

Amen.

[1] Okay, so you want to know his name – it's King Sekhemre-sementawy Djehuty. Try pronouncing that in public!

TRUE STORIES

A SWEET SOUND
IN YOUR EAR

This is Catherine Aldridge's own story of how she was healed of partial deafness when she was nine. It was written down in 1993 when she was eighteen and at University.

◆ THEME
Healing: a true story.

◆ YOU WILL NEED
- a bar of chocolate
- a Bible: *Mark 7:31-37*; a child to read it

◆ PRESENTATION
For an attention-grabbing opening, ask for a volunteer who would like to earn, say, a chocolate-bar. Have an adult place her hands firmly over the volunteer's ears and say to her in a normal voice eg, "I will give you this chocolate bar if you can tell me the name of the Prime Minister." Play on the volunteer's bafflement a moment or two before allowing her to hear others calling out the answer. Give her the reward, and talk briefly about the problems of deafness.

Have a child read the account of Jesus healing the deaf-mute in *Mark 7:31-37*. Then tell Catherine's story.

"Until I was nine I was partially deaf in both ears. This caused me many problems, especially in school. The classroom noise made hearing and understanding extremely difficult. As a child I loved to sing but, due to my deafness, I was completely unable to hear tunes or sing them back properly. Countless visits to the doctor didn't help to improve my hearing.

I used to go to church with my parents. One Sunday we found ourselves at a healing service. Although they knew the stories in the Bible about Jesus healing people, my parents had never thought of taking me for prayer. God had other ideas!

As people went to the front of the church to be prayed for, the music group was playing songs. They began to sing one which ends, "let it be a sweet, sweet sound in your ear". My parents turned to each other, wondering whether to take me forward. At the same time, my eleven-year-old brother was flicking through his Bible. Suddenly he said,

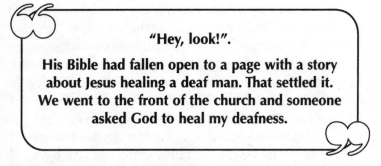

"Hey, look!".

His Bible had fallen open to a page with a story about Jesus healing a deaf man. That settled it. We went to the front of the church and someone asked God to heal my deafness.

MY PARENTS WERE TALKING

Later on that day I was playing in our back room. My parents were talking in the kitchen, and they mentioned my name. I jumped up and ran to ask why they were talking about me. There was no way that with my level of deafness I could have heard them. My parents began to be curious.

The next morning I woke up by myself and was instantly mad that I had been left in bed. I went to tell my parents off for forgetting to wake me, but they were still in bed. It was still ages till our normal getting-up time. I had been woken up by the birds singing. They weren't singing any louder than usual, it was simply that for the first time in my life I could hear them."

> Since then all my hearing tests have recorded perfect hearing in both ears. Singing has become something which I not only enjoy but also have a talent for. In fact, I now help lead the worship in church on Sunday mornings.
>
> What better way to use my talent than to praise the Lord and thank him for his healing!

✦ A SONG
Sing: *A Sweet Sound in Your Ear* (Songs of Fellowship, no 49 Book 1, Kingsway Publications 1981)

HEALED OF DYSLEXIA

✦ THEME
A remarkable true story.

✦ PRESENTATION
Ask the children if they know what dyslexia is. It is sometimes known as 'word-blindness'. Children suffering from dyslexia often fall behind at school and their frustration can lead to bad behaviour. Talk about the difficulties it causes. Then tell this story of Pat Carlin of Nottingham and the remarkable events which have happened in his life.

When Pat was born, he had spina bifida. There was a lump the size of a tennis ball at the base of his spine. Doctors said he would never walk without braces or crutches.

Spina bifida patients have fluid on the brain. This makes the head swell and an operation is needed to relieve the pressure. At that time a valve was usually put in the head to drain off the fluid, but at the last moment the doctors decided to try a different experimental operation on baby Pat. It was so new that they did not try this operation on anyone else for five or six years.

Every six months Pat had to be taken back to hospital for check-ups. The operation was clearly a success, as Pat was actually in advance of normal development for children of his age. He was the first child with spina bifida who walked naturally, without braces or other aids.

DYSLEXIA DIAGNOSED
The bad news was that Pat was very slow in learning to read. By the time he left Junior school he could only read as

well as most six year olds. At Secondary school they said he was dyslectic and he was sent for special teaching.

When he was twelve, Pat started going to church. He wasn't religious, he just wanted to earn some pocket-money! He joined the church choir and was paid to sing in Sunday services. He thought the people in church were off their rockers believing what they did, but he kept going because he wanted the money.

But gradually he began to think there might be something in it after all. When he was seventeen, he prayed in bed one night,

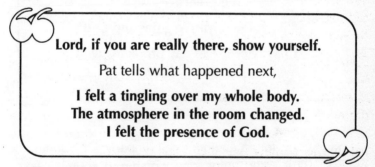

Lord, if you are really there, show yourself.

Pat tells what happened next,

**I felt a tingling over my whole body.
The atmosphere in the room changed.
I felt the presence of God.**

A few years later, Pat started going to some big Christian conferences. He heard about people being healed of different illnesses and he wondered if he could be healed of dyslexia. One autumn he went to a special healing service in his local church. It was to turn out to be a remarkable evening.

SHUT UP AND RECEIVE
The guest preacher prayed for several people. He was just about to finish when he said, "Is there anyone here with

word-blindness?" Pat was out to the front like a shot. He says,

> The preacher started praying for me.
> I was praying too, but he said, "Shut up, and just receive." Then he opened a Bible in the middle of the Old Testament, handed it to me, and said, "Read that."
>
> I was shocked, because I was able to read it and say it straight out without thinking about it. The preacher said,
>
> "Slow down, you're going too fast!"
>
> I have never had any problems with reading since.

Pat now works for an engineering company. On Sundays he plays his guitar and helps lead worship at church. Seeing him at work or at church, you would never know that he has struggled with both spina bifida and dyslexia.

SUFFERING DOESN'T STOP THE JOY

✦ THEME

The true story of a person who has suffered a great deal, but has retained a strong faith in God.

This is one man's personal experience, but it invites children to reflect on questions of suffering, of purpose, of where happiness is to be found, and of how faith can be the central reference point in someone's life.

✦ PRESENTATION

A suitable introduction might be to ask children how they think they might feel if they knew they were going to be confined to a wheelchair for the rest of their lives. How would they cope with constant pain and the knowledge that the pain was likely to get worse, not better?

One of the many people who has had to face those questions for real is Allan Tibble. Allan had been a miner in the Nottinghamshire coalfield for seven years when the accident happened. He was in an underground train on the way to the coal-face when the train stopped. Another locomotive ran into the back of the stationary train. Allan suffered a whiplash back injury which damaged his spine, nerves and muscles.

After four spells in hospital he was able to walk with a stick. But the doctors told him that the effects of the injury would get progressively worse. They were right. Within a couple of years, Allan needed a wheelchair to get around. He was – and is – in constant pain. Sometimes the pain gets so intense that he can't get out of the house for several days.

CHURCH WAS A KIND OF CLUB

As a child, Allan had been sent to Sunday School, but he stopped going as a teenager. When he met Christine, his future wife, he started going to church again. He believed in God, but not God as a person, more as an unknown something, a force out there, something in control. He thought being a Christian meant simply doing no-one any harm and doing a bit of good. Church was a kind of club where you met nice people. He began to help with the Boys Brigade.

But the pain in his back kept getting worse. He started blaming God.

"Why me? I don't deserve this. Other people have done much worse things than me."

He got angry, mad at God, unsure if he was really there.

Gradually Allan realised that there was no point blaming God or anyone else. Instead he started asking God for help. Several times he went to services where people prayed for him to be healed, but nothing happened.

THE BIG CHANGE

Allan tells when the turning point came. In his own words: "The big change came one night. And it was purely God."

"It was a really bad night. I was praying, "Please, God, take this pain away." I was making promises I knew I probably couldn't keep. Then it just came into my mind to ask for help to bear it, to face it, to deal with it, not to take it away."

As soon as Allan handed the problem over in this way, the answer came immediately. He felt a kind of warmth all over. The nearest way he can describe it is like being in the physiotherapy pool at the hospital – surrounded and supported on all sides; a gentle, soothing warmth. The pain didn't seem to matter so much.

It was the first time he fully realized that God was personal, real, alive - not a force or a thing. "From then on," says Allan, "he was a friend. And friends can help, especially a friend with that sort of power."

A VERY IMPORTANT MESSAGE

Allan is still in his wheelchair, known to thousands of children in the schools he visits for assemblies in his home town. The fact that he can't walk doesn't prevent him from showing the joy he has inside him that comes from God. Allan believes that just seeing him in his chair gives people a very important message: that suffering doesn't stop the joy.

He firmly believes that whatever is given to God will work out. No matter how bad you feel, it's not possible to be totally miserable. He is quite sure that one day he will be walking again - it might be on earth, or it might be in heaven; it doesn't matter which. But in his own words:

> I know one day I'm going to be walking alongside Jesus. He won't be pushing the chair - I'll be walking!

Allan Tibble is part of the CENS Assembly Team in Arnold, Nottingham.

GUIDELINES FOR GOOD COMMUNICATORS

AVOID THE HARD SELL

How many of us have the courage to simply tell a story or give an illustration and then walk away, leaving our hearers to work it out for themselves? Yet Jesus did it all the time. According to his historians, he never spoke to the crowds without using parables. His puzzled inner circle of followers sometimes had to badger him afterwards for explanations.

Jesus clearly wanted people to think things through, come to their own conclusions, and respond at their own pace. He knew that a free response is of infinitely greater value than a coerced response. I find that a hard act to follow!

At the very least, we can resist the temptation to deliver the 'moral' with hammer blows. Try finishing with a question rather than a statement; or by saying, "That's my opinion. What do you think?"

Allow stories like HEALED OF DYSLEXIA to speak for themselves. We can severely weaken the impact of a story by spinning lots of words or trying to re-inforce the message. It requires trust. But that is the way the Master did it.

ANDREW'S LAST WORDS

✦ THEME

We tend to shy away from talking about death with children, and yet it is vital that it should not be a taboo subject. This account of the last hours and words of Andrew Pickering contains much that is positive and full of hope.

✦ YOU WILL NEED

- the CD or cassette of the educational musical **Who is this Jesus?** (see page 192) which includes *Andrew's Song.*

✦ PRESENTATION

It is always a tragedy when a child dies. Nothing can take away the grief of the family. Thoughts and questions like, 'Why?' and 'Where was God?' are bound to come.

That was as true of the death of eight-year-old Andrew Pickering as of any other child.

But Andrew's last words were so strange that they made front-page news and are echoing around the world.

Andrew was a wonderful character, kind and courageous. He took life seriously, and yet was always full of fun. One of the great loves of his life was buses. He knew all the local Nottingham City buses just by the sound of their engines.

On his eighth birthday, the City bus drivers sent a double-decker to collect Andrew and his friends. They treated them to lunch at one bus depot and tea at another with lots of visits in between.

After his death, a special bus was named in his honour.

It was just before Easter 1994 that Andrew died after a long battle with leukemia. In his last few hours, at home with his parents, Andrew drifted in and out of consciousness many times. He wasn't feeling any pain, and seemed relaxed and happy. At one time he talked about being in a snow-storm. At another, he made noises that sounded like he was enjoying a ride on a Big Dipper.

He finally roused himself and spoke to his father one last time. What he said has made a great impression on many people. He said,

> **Don't blame Jesus, Dad. It's not his fault.**

People often do blame Jesus or God when tragedies happen. They say things like, "Why did God let this happen?" or "If God is all-powerful, why couldn't he stop this?"

> **Did Andrew meet Jesus as he was dying?**
>
> **Are his last words a message to the world?**

We can't be sure. But a song was written based on those words. The first verse and chorus goes like this:

There's a bomb blast in Egypt
A murder in Leeds
And a riot in Germany, too
There's an earthquake in India
A fire in L.A.
And what in the world can we do?

Don't blame Jesus
He suffered violence and shame
Don't blame Jesus
It was only for love that he came
He isn't the one you should blame.

That song became the climax of a musical based on the life of Jesus. When it was performed by 300 school children before audiences of over 4,000 people, Andrew's parents were guests of honour. As the first notes of *Andrew's Song* were played, a deep hush came over the audience. They had read Andrew's last words in the newspaper headline on the anniversary of his death two days before the show. Many people were in tears.

✦ A SONG
Play *Andrew's Song* from the CD or tape of **Who is this Jesus?**

That song has already gone to Africa, Australia, America, Lebanon and other countries. Many children in Britain are learning it as they take part in the musical. Andrew's courage as he faced leukemia impressed many people. The message of his last words is set to impress many more.

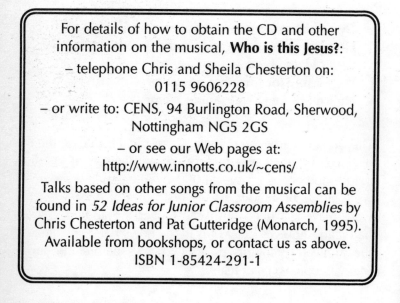

For details of how to obtain the CD and other information on the musical, **Who is this Jesus?**:

– telephone Chris and Sheila Chesterton on:
0115 9606228

– or write to: CENS, 94 Burlington Road, Sherwood, Nottingham NG5 2GS

– or see our Web pages at:
http://www.innotts.co.uk/~cens/

Talks based on other songs from the musical can be found in *52 Ideas for Junior Classroom Assemblies* by Chris Chesterton and Pat Gutteridge (Monarch, 1995). Available from bookshops, or contact us as above.
ISBN 1-85424-291-1

ADVENT AND CHRISTMAS

PREPARING FOR A BABY

✦ **THEME**
God made careful preparations for the coming of Jesus. An Advent talk.

✦ **YOU WILL NEED**
• ideally, a Mum who has recently had (or is about to have) a baby and who would be willing to talk to the children about preparations for a baby

✦ **PRESENTATION**
Talk about the preparations needed for a baby: the planning, the things to buy, maybe getting a room ready. If a Mum is not available, children who have recently had baby brothers or sisters might tell about some of the preparations in their families.

The season of Advent is the time before Christmas when we think about the coming of the baby Jesus. What plans did God make for Jesus? Here are some of the things he prepared:

• **The right family**. *Matthew 1:1* tells us that Jesus was "a descendant of David". David was the greatest of the kings of Israel. For many years people had been expecting someone very special to come, the Messiah. They knew he would be a member of David's family.

• **The right people**. Jesus was also 'a descendant of Abraham.' The Jewish people called themselves 'sons of Abraham'. They were a nation with a long history of knowing God and his ways and of looking forward to the coming Messiah.

- **The right place**. 700 years before Jesus was born the prohet Micah had said that the Messiah would be born in Bethlehem. (*Micah 5:2*) Bethlehem was King David's home town.

- **The right herald** to tell people he was coming. This was Jesus' cousin, John the Baptist. (*Luke 1:76*)

- **Witnesses**: the shepherds and the Wise Men. They saw where Jesus was born and could tell of the strange events that led them there.

- **The right time**. Jesus was born at the time that 'the Roman Emperor Augustus ordered a census to be taken throughout the Roman Empire' (*Luke 2:1*). News spread quickly through Roman Empire with its good roads and frequent travellers. It was the ideal setting for the Christian message to be carried far and wide.

These preparations took a long time. David was king 1000 years before Jesus was born. For the Jewish people it must have seeemed as though the Messiah would never come. Nine months is a long time to wait for a Mum expecting a baby. But it is an exciting time, just like the weeks leading up to Christmas. It was a long wait for the Messiah, but it was exciting for those who recognised him when he did come.

✦ **A SONG**
While Shepherds Watched Their Flocks by Night.

Note verse 3:   "To you in David's town, this day
                       Is born, of David's line,
                       A Saviour, who is Christ the Lord. ..."

CHRISTMAS FAITH 1
F IS FOR FATHER

This is the first of a series of six talks explaining the meaning of the word faith in the context of Christmas. The first five are based on words beginning with the letters of FAITH and the last sums up the whole series and invites a response. Each is accompanied by an appropriate carol.

✦ THEME
Faith is in a person, God the Father.

✦ YOU WILL NEED
- five large boxes wrapped in Christmas paper with cut-outs of one of the letters F A I T H on each.

- a Bible. Prepare to briefly retell the story of Lazarus in *John 11:17-45*.
- music for *O Come All Ye Faithful*, or a recording.

✦ PRESENTATION
Play or sing the first verse of *O Come All Ye Faithful*. This famous carol invites people who are faithful to come and worship the baby Jesus. Faithful means 'full of faith', but what is faith?

Show your Christmas boxes with the letters on them.

> **For Christians, faith is always in someone, in a person. That someone is God.**

Jesus always talked about God as his Father, so on this first box the F stands for Father.

Jesus had an earthly father, Joseph. He was a good man, but even the best earthly fathers can let us down. Jesus knew that his heavenly Father would never let him down.

Let's look at an example from his later life of how Jesus had faith in his heavenly Father. Retell the story of the raising of Lazarus from *John 11:17-45*. Focus on verses 41-42:

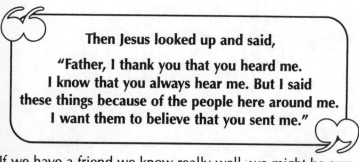

> **Then Jesus looked up and said,**
>
> **"Father, I thank you that you heard me.
> I know that you always hear me. But I said
> these things because of the people here around me.
> I want them to believe that you sent me."**

If we have a friend we know really well, we might be sure they will not let us down. Jesus knew his heavenly Father so well that he could say, "I know that you always hear me." That is faith. And Jesus wanted the people around him to have that same faith in God as their heavenly Father.

✦ A SONG
O Come All Ye Faithful

CHRISTMAS FAITH 2
T IS FOR TRUST

✦ THEME
A vital element of faith is trust.

✦ YOU WILL NEED
- the five F A I T H Christmas present boxes
- a bottle a coloured water (use food colouring) with a label saying 'MEDICINE' and a spoon.
- a Bible: *Luke 1:26-45*. This could be given to a group of children to prepare as a dramatised reading.
- music for *Once in Royal David's City*.

✦ PRESENTATION
Show the box with the T on it. T stands for Trust, one of the most important parts of faith.

Ask for a volunteer who has been to the doctor's recently. Show her the bottle of medicine.

> **If the doctor had asked her to take a spoonful of something like this, would she have taken it? ... If a stranger had come up to her in the street and said the same thing, would she have taken it then? ...**

What is the difference? – Trust.

Retell or present as a dramatised reading *Luke 1:26-45*, the story of the angel Gabriel's message to Mary.

Bring out Mary's fear and lack of understanding. Despite this, Mary trusted – verse 36.

Show the box with the F on it. Last time we said that the important thing is that it is faith in a person. Who is that person? – God the Father. Because it was God (through an angel) who spoke to her, Mary was able to trust that he would not let her down.

> **Can we trust him like Mary did?**

✦ **A SONG**
Once in Royal David's city.

CHRISTMAS FAITH 3
A IS FOR ACTION

✦ THEME
In James' words, 'Faith by itself, if is it not accompanied by action, is dead.'

✦ YOU WILL NEED
- the five F A I T H Christmas present boxes
- a milk bottle full of water and a piece of card a little larger than the mouth of the bottle. See the text below and try the demonstration at home first to convince yourself that it works.
- a towel in case of disasters!
- a Bible: *Matthew 2:1-12*
- music for *As With Gladness* or *The First Nowell*.

✦ PRESENTATION
Show the box with the A on it. A stands for Action. Last time we looked at T for Trust. Now we are going to see if someone trusts enough to put their trust into action.

Fill a milk bottle with water leaving no more than a few millimetres air-space. Place a fresh, flat piece of card over the top. Tell children that if you turn the bottle upside-down the card will stay in place and no water will come out (except possibly the odd drop). This is not a trick, just simple science. It is the effect of air-pressure. Who believes you? ... Who is prepared to put that trust into action by standing underneath the bottle as you turn it upside-down? ...

Choose a volunteer, hold the card in place as you turn the bottle upside-down, count to three and release the card. The water remains in the bottle. (Well, this series is about faith!)

Read, retell or get children to read *Matthew 2:1-12,* the visit of the Wise Men or scholars. These men put their faith into action in at least three ways. One: they said, 'We saw his star in the east and have come to worship him.' Two: they had come prepared with gifts. Three: they acted on the warning dream at the end of the story.

> See how when the Wise Men acted in faith, the proof came afterwards.
>
> Faith may be a step into the unknown, but once the step is taken it can be seen to be right.

The Wise Men not only saw the Christ-child, they were 'overjoyed' (v.10). If they hadn't put their belief into action they would have missed out on the proof that they were right. And they would have missed out on the excitement and the joy.

✦ **A SONG**
As With Gladness or *The First Nowell.*

CHRISTMAS FAITH 4
I IS FOR INCARNATION

✦ THEME
At Christmas we meet God 'in the flesh'.

NOTE Although we try to avoid using jargon, especially when talking to children, it is good practice to introduce longer or harder words like 'incarnation' from time to time.

✦ YOU WILL NEED
- the five F A I T H Christmas present boxes
- a Bible: *Luke 2:8-20*.
- somebody who can talk about a famous person they met or a couple of people to prepare a spoof interview with a famous person or photos from a pop-music or sports magazine.
- music for *Hark the Herald Angels Sing* or *Love Came Down at Christmas*.

✦ PRESENTATION
Show the box with the I on it. I stands for Incarnation. It is a long word. What does it mean?

Intoduce the person who has met somebody famous, or the sketch, or show the pop-idol or sports photos and ask the children if they have ever met one of their heroes. We talk about meeting somebody 'in the flesh'. It is very different – and exciting – meeting someone you've only known on a TV screen 'in the flesh'.

That is exactly what the word 'incarnation' means: 'in the flesh' or 'in a human body'.

People like Mary and the Wise Men knew God and trusted in him even though they had never seen him. The great excitement of the first Christmas was that they met him for the first time 'in the flesh', in a human body.

Read or retell or have children read the story of the shepherds in *Luke 2:8-20*.

Stress verses 11-12. This is 'a Saviour ... Christ the Lord' ; the angel Gabriel had told Mary he was 'the Son of God', and yet he had come as a baby. This is what Christians call 'the incarnation', God come into the world in the flesh, in a human body.

> From this moment on, faith for those who would later be called Christians was not just faith in God the Father, it was-and still is – faith in God the Son, God in a human body.

✦ **A SONG**
Hark the Herald Angels Sing or *Love Came Down at Christmas.*

CHRISTMAS FAITH 5
H IS FOR HOLY

✦ THEME
Holiness is to be experienced.

✦ YOU WILL NEED
- the five F A I T H Christmas present boxes
- candles and matches
- music for *Silent Night*.

✦ PRESENTATION
Show the box with the H on it. H stands for Holy. It's a word that comes up a lot in the Christmas story and in Christmas carols: *Silent night, holy night*.

Play the music of *Silent Night*. (It would be very effective to continue playing the music quietly in the background while talking about aspects of experiencing holiness.)

When the angel Gabriel comes to Mary, he tells her about 'the holy one to be born'. When Mary sings a song of praise to God she says, 'for the Mighty One has done great things for me – holy is his name.'

> **What does 'holy' mean?**

You can't really explain what 'holy' means, you can only experience it. Perhaps the best way is to imagine ourselves at the first Christmas with Mary and Joseph, the angels, the shepherds and the Wise Men. When we sing carols, especially at a candlelit carol service, it can help us imagine what it felt like to be there.

One of the things people feel is that this is a very special moment, perhaps the most special moment you will ever know in your whole life. The Wise Men were clever scholars, but the Bible says that they 'bowed down and worshipped' this baby of a poor family. They knew this baby came from God. It is only God who is holy, or things or people that belong to God.

Another thing people feel and know without being told is that they are in the presence of someone pure and completely good. This goodness is so pefect that it can only come from God. Would you swear or quarrel or lie if you came to see Jesus in the manger? No, you would just feel that that would be utterly wrong.

A third thing people feel is that they are in the presence of a mystery. They feel that there is something which is bigger than human understanding. We can't fully understand God incarnate, God in a human body. We can't fully grasp how or why. We can only marvel. After the shepherds left the Bible says that 'Mary treasured up all these things and pondered them in her heart'. She pondered them; they were a mystery.

People who have been in the presence of holiness feel tremendously privileged and very humble. They are filled with deep peace and joy.

This was the experience of all those who came into the presence of the baby Jesus at that first Christmas.

It was the faith of the shepherds and the Wise Men and Mary and Joseph that led them to this place. And being close to 'the holy one' made their faith far, far deeper. When people have an experience like this, they remember it all their lives and it becomes a very important part of them.

✦ A SONG
Light some candles and sing *Silent Night*.

Children might be informed of a candlelit carol service they could attend.

CHRISTMAS FAITH 6
A GIFT

✦ **THEME**
Summing up: faith is a gift.

✦ **YOU WILL NEED**
- the five F A I T H Christmas present boxes
- music for *O Little Town of Bethlehem*.

✦ **PRESENTATION**
Play or sing a verse of *O Little Town of Bethlehem*.

Display the five boxes. Remind children of the aspects of faith these letters stand for. F is for God the Father in whom Christians put their faith. A is for the Action that shows that faith is genuine. I is for Incarnation, God in a human body, Jesus in whom Christians also put their faith. T is for Trust, the trust in God that leads to action. H is for Holy, the holiness that people may experience as a result of their faith – and which leads to even deeper faith.

The first lines of the third verse of *O Little Town of Bethlehem* read: 'How silently, how silently, The wondrous gift is given!' The gift the carol speaks of is the gift of Jesus, the Christ, to the world.

> These boxes wrapped in Christmas paper remind us that faith is also a gift. This gift is given quietly to those who want to receive it. There are many people in the world who would say it is the most precious gift they have ever received.

Mother Teresa puts it like this:

> **In India I was asked by some government people, "Don't you want to make us all Christians?"**
>
> **I said, "Naturally, I would like to give the treasure I have to you, but I cannot. I can only pray for you to have the courage to receive it."**
>
> **Faith is a gift from God.** [1]

As people all over the world sing *O Little Town of Bethlehem* this Christmas, many of them will use the last verse as a prayer, asking God to renew and deepen their faith once again:

O holy child of Bethlehem,
Descend to us we pray;
Cast out our sin and enter in;
Be born in us today.

That prayer is open for anyone to pray if they wish.

✦ A SONG
Sing *O Little Town of Bethlehem.*

[1] Mother Teresa, *Loving Jesus*, Fount (London 1991) p.100.

GUIDELINES FOR GOOD COMMUNICATORS

DON'T PATRONISE

It is better not to talk to children at all than to talk down to them.

Christmas is one of those times when it is easy to slip into 'This is for the children' mode. In fact there are very few messages for children in the Bible. There is only truth for all people. And all people have to come as children before our Father in heaven.

Children ask big questions and are capable of wrestling with difficult ideas. Our task is to find the language and the pictures which will help them in their thinking.

CHRISTMAS FAITH 4 introduces the concept of the incarnation. The incarnation is all about God coming alongside us in the form of Jesus and finding the words and pictures to communicate to us. As I read the Gospels and see Jesus doing this I feel uplifted, never patronised.

Here are two ways of avoiding being patronising. One is an attitude, the other a technique.

The right attitude when talking to children is knowing that to do so is an awesome privilege. Each one of them is a precious and unique creation who will one day, God willing, be a being in a world outside space and time and beyond our present comprehension. To be responsible for helping them take a step on that journey – or for hindering them by our own pride or folly – is a humbling responsibility.

The technique is one to be used when talking to a wide age-range of children: aim for the oldest. Providing the talk is entertaining or has good visual elements, it will hold the younger ones' attention. If they don't understand everything but are left with a sense that there are good things for them to grow into, that's fine. It is much better than the older ones feeling that this is all beneath them and that they have already grown out of Christianity.

CHRISTMAS PRESENT FROM AFAR

✦ **THEME**
God's goodness in sending Jesus into the world.

✦ **YOU WILL NEED**
- two Christmas stockings, an old-fashioned one with nuts, an orange and a small toy, and one with some electronic wizardry from Japan such as a personal stereo or game cartridge

✦ **PRESENTATION**
Show your old-fashioned stocking. Talk about the contents and how an orange would have been an exotic treat for a previous generation.

Ask what children are hoping for this Christmas. Some will want Playstations, Saturn, etc, or new games for their existing sets. Display the contents of your second stocking. Point out how popular items come from Japan, thousands of miles away around the world.

A return flight to Japan costs between £500 and £1000. If parents had to go to Japan to buy these presents, how many children think they would be getting them for Christmas? Not many! Isn't it a good job importers bring them over for us at a fraction of that cost!

For thousands of years, people all over the world have believed that the most important thing in life is to know the Creator of the universe and to be right with him. But if he is the Creator, he is 'outside', 'beyond' the universe he made. How do we find out what he is like? We might make some good guesses, but how do we really know? Travelling to

Japan for Christmas presents is too much for most parents. Going 'outside' the universe is too much for anyone!

But the Christmas story tells us we don't have to. The Christmas story says that God came to us. One of the names given to Jesus was 'Immanuel'. It means, 'God with us'.

There is a line in the well-loved carol, *Once In Royal David's City* – 'He came down to earth from heaven Who is God and Lord of all'.

> **From heaven to earth: that is an infinite distance, impossible for people to cross.**
> **But God loves us so much he sent Jesus to earth as his Christmas present to the world.**

✦ **A SONG**
Once In Royal David's City

WISE MEN
UNRAVEL CLUES

✦ **THEME**

A Christmas detective story.

✦ **YOU WILL NEED**

- nothing essential, but a crib or picture of the Wise Men would be helpful

✦ **PRESENTATION**

We all know the Christmas story of the Wise Men, but have you ever thought of them as detectives, unravelling clues and seeking information to find the hidden birthplace of the Messiah, the promised King of the Jews?

The first clue they might have seen was in 7 BC. Three times that year the planets Jupiter and Saturn passed close to each other in the constellation of Pisces. To ancient star-gazers this was significant. Jupiter was the king of the planets, Saturn stood for the Messiah, and Pisces was the constellation of the Jews. Our wise detectives could have seen this as a sign that the Messiah, the King of the Jews, was coming.

(By the way, seeing a sign in the sky of a very special event is different from reading your 'stars' in a newspaper. Astrology says that the stars influence the way people behave. The Bible says that is wrong and modern research has totally disproved it.).

Two years later, in 5 BC, Chinese records tell of a bright comet that was visible in the sky for more than seventy days. Could that have been the Christmas star that led prompted the Wise Men to set out on their quest? A professor at Cambridge University thinks it was [1].

Hold on a minute! Wasn't Jesus born in 1 AD? Surely 5 BC is far too early. Well, probably not. A sixth century monk made a mistake in calculating the date of the birth of Jesus. (It's nice to know grown-ups can get their maths wrong, too!) Who was king when Jesus was born? ... King Herod. Herod died in 4 BC. So the most likely date for the birth of Jesus is in 5 BC.

Anyway, back to our detectives. They were looking for the Messiah, the King of the Jews. Where to begin their search was easy: Jerusalem, the capital city of the Jews. So they arrived in Jerusalem asking questions,

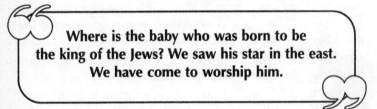

Where is the baby who was born to be the king of the Jews? We saw his star in the east. We have come to worship him.

It didn't take long for King Herod's secret service to get wind of these strangers and their questions. In no time a worried Herod had called a meeting of experts, his own wise men. If it was the Messiah, where would he be born? The experts had the answer to that. More than 700 years earlier, a man called Micah had made a prophecy, a prediction, about the Messiah.

This is what he said: (Preferably read this direct from a Bible – *Micah 5:2*)

> **But you, Bethlehem Ephrathah, are one
> of the smallest towns in Judah. But from you
> will come one who will rule Israel for me.
> He comes from very old times,
> from days long ago.**

Bethlehem, that was the answer. If there was any truth in this king of the Jews thing, Herod wasn't the kind of man to sit back and allow a rival on the scene. After all, he had already killed other people who were threats to the throne. He called the Wise Men to a secret meeting and gave them the last clue they were looking for: Bethlehem was the place. Herod's plan was to use the Wise Men to find the baby and then get rid of it. But God had other plans!

The Wise Men set out the last few miles to Bethlehem. It says in the Bible that the star 'stopped over the place where the child was'. In ancient writings, words like 'stood over' usually refer to comets. It may mean that by the time they got to Bethlehem the comet's tail was vertical in the night sky. This would be the final confirmation to the Wise Men that they had found the right place. A few simple enquiries in the village would have led them to Mary and the baby Jesus. The rest is the story we all know from Christmas cards and Nativity plays.

Now, all this is a modern detective story, and nobody really knows whether these signs in the sky are the actual ones the Wise men saw.

But whatever they were, the Wise Men pieced them together and discovered both the right time and the right place. They found Jesus and worshipped him as the Messiah, the promised King of kings. Twenty centuries later, people all over the world are piecing together their own clues and still coming to the same conclusion: that Jesus is God's promised Messiah.

✦ A PRAYER

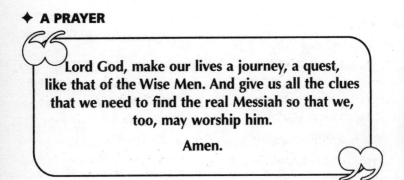

Lord God, make our lives a journey, a quest, like that of the Wise Men. And give us all the clues that we need to find the real Messiah so that we, too, may worship him.

Amen.

[1] Professor Colin Humphreys.

EASTER AND PENTECOST

GOOD FRIDAY RIDDLE

✦ THEME
God's love and justice meet in Good Friday.

✦ YOU WILL NEED
- a few centimetres of milk in a bottle that has been left out a couple of days to go obviously sour.
- an unopened carton of UHT milk
- 2 glasses
- a cross

✦ PRESENTATION
Today we are going to think about a riddle, and how Good Friday is the answer. You meet the riddle when you think about heaven. If someone says about something, "That was heaven!", what do they mean? ... It was just perfect.

We may not all believe in heaven, and none of us knows what it is like, but one thing we can probably all agree on is that heaven must be perfect. No crime, no hunger, no injustice, no suffering.

> **Now, hands up everyone who is perfect ...**
> **Who has never told a lie? ...**
> **Never taken a biscuit when mum said not to? ...**
> **Never been nasty to someone else? ...**

Okay, so none of us is perfect. What would that do for heaven if God lets us in? ... It would no longer be perfect because we would be in it and we are not perfect!

A DRINK OF SOUR MILK

Let's think about something entirely different for a moment: milk. Open the carton of UHT milk and offer a drink to a volunteer. Now offer someone else a drink of sour milk. Yuk!

What is the difference? How long will UHT milk keep unopened? Why? ... Pasteurising milk kills most of the bacteria, but enough are left to turn the milk sour after a few days. UHT milk is sterilised to kill all the bacteria.

We have all admitted to being less than perfect. We may not be out and out evil, but we all have the 'bacteria' of wrong-doing in us. If God let us into heaven, would it still be perfect? Or would we 'infect' it? If I pour this sour milk into this UHT milk, what will happen? ... It will all go sour.

So here is the riddle. It looks as if the situation is this:

1. God made us and told us about heaven.

2. He also gave us the ability to choose between right and wrong.

3. We all make mistakes and do wrong things. None of us is perfect.

4. But heaven is perfect – so none of us can go to heaven. **Goodbye, get lost!**

Does that make you want to shout, "Unfair!"? ... Right. But the Bible tells us this about God: he is holy (everything about him is perfect); he is just (he can't stand unfairness); and he is love. Because he is all those things, God provided an answer to the riddle. The answer is Good Friday. (Show the cross.)

GOD'S GOODNESS POURED INTO US

Christians believe that Jesus was perfect. He was sinless. But listen to how St Paul explains what happened on Good Friday when Jesus was crucified:

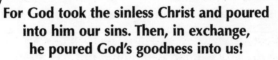

For God took the sinless Christ and poured into him our sins. Then, in exchange, he poured God's goodness into us!

2 Corinthians 5:21, Living Bible

Jesus was pure, sinless. (Hold up UHT milk.) God poured our sins into him. (Hold up sour milk.) The difference between Jesus and milk is that our 'bacteria' did not infect him. Then, having totally cleaned us out, he poured his goodness, his perfection, into us. In his love, he makes us fit for heaven. The riddle is solved at Good Friday.

That is why Christians celebrate the crucifixion of Jesus – and why we all have a holiday.

✦ A PRAYER

Father God, there are many riddles and puzzles in life. We ask you show us the answers to the important ones. Amen.

✦ THEME
The meaning of Good Friday

✦ YOU WILL NEED
- nothing, unless you want to make a list as a visual aid (see end of sixth paragraph)

✦ PRESENTATION
Here is a question for the days leading up to Easter:

> **Why is a woman who could not pay a fine for not having a TV licence like Good Friday?**

The woman, Sharon Jones of Ebbw Vale, was expecting a baby one November when she had to go to court. She has six other children. She was sentenced to five days in jail for failing to pay a £55 pound fine for not having a TV licence. She broke down in tears when the sentence was passed. She was due to give birth in just two weeks.

One of the people in the court was a solicitor called Carole Anthony. (A solicitor helps people present their case if they have to go to court.) She was so moved by Mrs Jones' distress that she organised a collection among other solicitors present. Between them they raised the £55 for the fine and so saved Mrs Jones from having to go to prison.

Mrs Anthony said, **"Everyone felt sorry for this poor lady, so we very quietly put the money forward for the fine – it just seemed the right thing to do."**

WE OWED A DEBT

So why is that like Good Friday? Well, it says in the Bible that we all owe a fine that is too big for us to pay. St Paul puts it like this:

> **We owed a debt because we broke God's laws.**
> **That debt listed all the rules we failed to follow.**
>
> *Colossians 2:14a*

The ways we have all broken God's laws include how we treat each other and how we fail to care for the world God created for us. That adds up to a pretty long list for every one of us. (You could have a roll of paper purporting to have a list on it. Hold it up and let it unroll.)

But Paul goes on:

> **But God forgave us that debt.**
> **He took away that debt and nailed it to the cross.**
>
> *Col. 2:14b*

The debt we owed, the fine that is too big for us to pay, was nailed to the cross with Jesus. As Paul says,

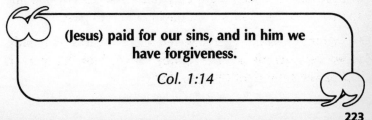

> **(Jesus) paid for our sins, and in him we**
> **have forgiveness.**
>
> *Col. 1:14*

This is why the Friday on which Christians remember the crucifixion of Jesus is called 'Good'. Every Christian remembers the list of things he or she has done wrong, the debt he cannot pay, to God. He remembers how he has said sorry for those things and admitted that there is no way he can pay the fine. He has asked Jesus to pay it for him.

If you can imagine how Sharon Jones felt when that fine was paid and she was saved from prison, then you can get a sense of what every Christian feels. That is a good reason for calling Good Friday 'Good'!

✦ SOMETHING TO THINK ABOUT
The children could imagine their list and what might be on it. Have they given that list to Jesus to be nailed to the Cross? Do they want to?

(The story of Sharon Jones appeared in the press on 26.11.'93.)

AN UNUSUAL
FRENCH CROSS

In homes and churches in parts of the French Alps you can sometimes see a fascinating cross decorated with symbols representing different parts of the crucifixion story. The drawing is based on one such in a tiny chapel in the hamlet of Les Cours, near the Col du Lautaret (a regular stage of the Tour de France). It is a good teaching aid, and one we can easily copy for either a single talk or a series.

✦ THEME
The story of Good Friday.

✦ YOU WILL NEED
- a copy of the drawing on OHP acetate *or* start with a bare cross on paper or an OHP and add different elements *or* a group of children might make their own version out of wood or card and scrap materials.
- a Bible. Most of these elements of the story can be found in John's account of the crucifixion, chapters 18 and 19 of *John's Gospel*. Other references are given below.

✦ PRESENTATION
Tell the story pointing to or adding the various elements. Depending on the amount of detail, or the lessons one wants to draw, this could be a single talk or a short series.

The various elements are:

- **a coin** - one of the thirty pieces of silver paid to Judas for betraying Jesus

INRI

- **the cock** that crowed when Peter denied knowing Jesus for the third time

- **the whip** used to scourge Jesus

- **a hand** – one of Pilate's when he washed his hands of the guilt of Jesus' death (Matthew 27:24)

- **hammer, nails, ladder and pincers** used for fixing Jesus to the cross and later removing his body

- **INRI sign** – initial letters of Jesus of Nazareth, King of the Jews (Latin: Jesus Nazarenus Rex Judaeorum) which Pilate had fixed to the cross

- **a goblet and sponge on a stick** used to give Jesus a drink of sour wine

- **dice** used by the soldiers to gamble for Jesus' clothes (*Matthew 27:35*)

- **sun and moon** – darkness fell from mid-day to mid-afternoon (*Matthew 27:45*)

- **a spear** used to pierce Jesus' side to check whether he was dead

- **the Ten Commandments** – to symbolize the fact that Jesus' death satisfied the demands of the Law (*Romans 8:3-4*)

- **the heart** – to symbolize the love of God shown in Jesus' death (*1 John 3:16*)

GUIDELINES FOR GOOD COMMUNICATORS

CARRYING CONVICTION

'The best lack all conviction,' wrote Yeats, 'whilst the worse are full of passionate intensity.'

How do we convey conviction without putting our hearers off with the hard sell? How do we persuade a post-modern generation that what we believe is vitally relevant to them, too, and not just a personal choice of our own creation?

Perhaps the answer lies in having an attitutude modelled on that of Jesus as he talked to two of his followers on the road to Emmaus. This is the story featured in HARD TO RECOGNISE.

Jesus used their knowledge of the Hebrew scriptures (he started from where they were at) to lead them into understanding and to impart a burning conviction of truth to them. Then when they reached the village, 'Jesus acted as if he were going further'. It was their free choice to invite him to stay, and only after they had made that choice did he reveal his identity to them.

Each child we speak to has a God-given freedom to weigh what we say and to respond in their own time and their own way. (The parable of the sower has shown us in advance the broad outline of those responses.) We have to respect that freedom absolutely, just as Jesus did – even on the day of his resurrection.

So we use persuasion, not manipulation; truth, not enticement; the appeal of love, not the coercion of superiority. Then we pray that, like young Andrew Pickering in ANDREW'S LAST WORDS, the time will come for each one's eyes to be opened and that each will recognise Jesus as the risen Lord and Saviour.

HAR-DTOR-ECO-GNI-SE

✦ THEME
Introducing part of the Easter story, the road to Emmaus.

✦ YOU WILL NEED
- to prepare some words as in the examples below, taking the ability of the children into account.
- a Bible. Refresh your memory of the story of Jesus on the road to Emmaus in *Luke 24:13-35*.

✦ PRESENTATION
On acetates or sheets of paper, write out some words with the letters split into odd groups as in the examples below. Get some volunteers and ask them to read the words aloud. Show them one at a time. See how long it takes to recognise the words.

Examples: **too-thac-he, fi-rem-an, co-atho-ok, cha-ins-aw, frig-hte-ni-ng, my-sterio-us.**

To make it even more difficult, some might be written like this:

te

lep

ho

ned

Some people will find this very hard. Others might find they do not recognise the word at first, then suddenly they see it.

THE ROAD TO EMMAUS

There is a well-known Easter story about two friends who took quite a long time to recognise someone they knew very well. Fill in the background: this is the Sunday after Jesus was crucified and buried on the Friday. Tell the story of how Jesus appeared to two disciples on the road from Jerusalem to Emmaus. It is in *Luke 24:13-35*.

Make the connection with the introduction: a person or a word seen in an unexpected way or place may be hard to recognise at first. In this case they were sure Jesus was dead. Perhaps he wore a cloak with a hood, or perhaps in some way they were prevented from recognising him. One translation of verse 32 says,

> **And then, they were allowed to recognise Jesus.**

We have had some fun exercising our brains to play a game recognising words. How much more brain-stretching it was for these friends of Jesus as he told them all the things the Bible taught about him. And how much more exciting when the penny finally dropped and they realised it was Jesus risen from the dead who had been sharing their walk along the Emmaus road.

✦ TIME FOR REFLECTION

Play some quiet music. The children might like to replay this story in their minds, perhaps imagining themselves as one of the two disciples.

VICTORY CUP

✦ **THEME**
Reminders of victories won; the meaning of the communion cup.

✦ **YOU WILL NEED**
- a silver cup or other trophy that has been won by an individual or a team
- a glass of 'wine' (grape or blackcurrant juice) or a communion chalice if you can borrow one
- visual aid from *Put A Spoon In Your Shoe* (see below)

✦ **PRESENTATION**
(If you are using this subsequent to *Put A Spoon In Your Shoe*, show the rocks or the illustration or a shoe with a spoon in it and ask children what this reminds them of. Ask if children have tried out the idea and with what success.)

Show the cup or trophy and talk about it. This is a reminder – a reminder of a past victory.

Show the glass of 'wine' or chalice. This cup is also a reminder of a victory. To Christians it is a reminder of the most important victory of all.

On the night before he was crucified, Jesus shared what is often known as 'the last supper' with his friends. During that meal he took a cup of wine and passed it round the table for them all to drink. This is what he said:

"This cup shows the new agreement from God to his people. This new agreement begins with the blood of my death. When you drink this, do it to remember me."
(*1 Corinthians 11:25*)

Later that night he was arrested, tried and crucified. That sounds like a terrible defeat. But Christians believe it was the forces of evil in the world that were defeated, not Jesus. Paul put it like this a letter:

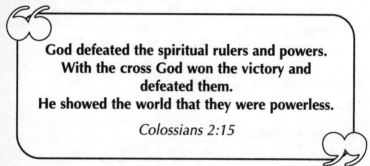

God defeated the spiritual rulers and powers. With the cross God won the victory and defeated them. He showed the world that they were powerless.

Colossians 2:15

Every Sunday all over the world – and often on weekdays, too – Christians do what Jesus told them to and take some bread and wine in the service known as the Mass or the Eucharist or Communion. As they do so, they remember how Jesus died and they celebrate the victory over evil.

This cup (show trophy) is a reminder of a past sports victory. It also encourages those who compete next time to try their hardest to win it. This cup [show wine] reminds people of the victory of Jesus over evil on the cross. It also encourages Christians to try their hardest to live in the way God wants, knowing what he has already done for them.

✦ SOMETHING TO DO

Can someone print out a picture of the bread and wine and Jesus' words in *1 Corinthians 11:25* on a computer? They could either draw the bread and wine or see if they can find some clip-art.

THE CHURCH'S BIRTHDAY

✦ **THEME**

Pentecost is the time to celebrate the Church's birthday.

✦ **YOU WILL NEED**

- a birthday cake, some candles, matches, and a taper if possible
- a Bible: *Acts 2:1-4*

✦ **PRESENTATION**

Show the cake. Today (or next Sunday) is someone's – or rather, something's – birthday. Anyone know whose? A clue: it is around 1970 years old. Answer: the Church. Not our church or St Wotsit's down the road, but the Church made up of all the followers of Jesus.

When we have a birthday cake, it is often brought in with the candles alight. Then the birthday person has to take a deep breath and blow them all out. The Church started with a strong breath and flames, but it was sort of the other way round.

Describe the coming of the Holy Spirit in *Acts 2:1-4*. Let the candles represent the followers of Jesus. Light a match or taper and bring it down onto the candles so that each one has a flame on its 'head'.

The flames of the Spirit were not blown out. Briefly describe the rest of the events of that day, culminating in three thousand people being baptised (*Acts 2:41*). The Church has gone on growing down the centuries. There are around one billion Christians in the world today. That's a lot of people to join in celebrating the Church's birthday!

SOMETHING TO ENJOY

With a small group, the cake can be cut and eaten. A church might decide to ask members to bring 'birthday' cakes to share after the service. If this message is used for a school assembly, take the cake to be eaten with coffee in the staffroom at break. This will ensure that it is a very popular assembly with the staff!

BREATH AND SPIRIT

✦ THEME
The surprising effect of the Spirit of God.

✦ YOU WILL NEED
- two table-tennis balls, some thread, sellotape, and a broom handle. Stick thread to two table-tennis balls with sticky tape and suspend them from a broom-handle across two chairs as in the illustration. Make the gap between the balls 6 - 7 cm. Raise high enough for your audience to see.
- a Bible. Prepare the two stories of Peter in *Luke 22:54-62* (his denial of Jesus) and *Acts 4:1-22* (Peter stands up fearlessly to the authorities) or arrange for a group of children to read these sections in *The Dramatised Bible* (published by Marshall Pickering / The Bible Society).

✦PRESENTATION
Show the 'apparatus' you have prepared for a small experiment. If you blow on one of the table-tennis balls, will it move towards you or away? ... Obviously, away.

If you blow between the two balls, will they move away from each other or towards each other? ... Demonstrate. They move towards each other. Why? ... Air moving over a curved surface drops in pressure, creating 'lift'. This is what keeps a plane up in the sky: air moving over the curved upper surface of the wing pulls it – and the plane – upwards. Air moving over the table-tennis balls pulls them towards the side over which your breath is blowing.

Refer to the story of Pentecost and the sound like rushing wind (*Acts 2:1-2*). The Spirit of God came on the followers of Jesus in power. The word for 'spirit' in the original language is the same as the word for 'breath'.

When you breathe – or the wind blows – you can't see the air moving, but you can see it's effects. The table-tennis balls experiment is one example. It is the same with the Spirit of God. You can't see him (although the disciples saw something that looked like fire), but you can see the effect he has in people's lives. Just as with the table-tennis balls, that effect can often be quite surprising.

Briefly tell the 'before and after' stories of Peter in *Luke 22:54-62* and *Acts 4:1-22*. Draw attention to *Acts 4:8* – Peter was 'filled with the Holy Spirit' – and v.13 - 'they saw the courage of Peter and ... were astonished'.

✦ **A PRAYER**

Holy Spirit, come and breathe on us.
Change us like you changed Peter. Do things in our lives that will astonish people. Amen.

PENTECOST RAP

✦ THEME
Re-telling the story of the day of Pentecost in a modern idiom.

✦ YOU WILL NEED
- copies of the text. This is best performed by a group of children. When reading or reciting this rap, emphasise the rhythm. It can be accompanied by finger-snapping 4 beats to the line. Insert a line of finger-snapping between stanzas, or get a percussionist to play a link.
- copy or photocopy the illustrations of Art Simple onto acetate – there is one to accompany each stanza. Get someone to practise showing the correct ones to accompany the rap.

  OR designate one of the group as Art to mime responses.

✦ PRESENTATION
The Jews celebrate the feast of Pentecost, also known as the Feast of Weeks, seven weeks after Passover. It is the time for celebrating the grain harvest. For Christians, the day is also very important because of what happened after the first Easter. Here is the story of the events told in a rap with the help of a character called Art Simple.

Now get your mind in gear and don't wander or get lost,
Here's a real solid tale about the day of Pentecost.
To keep us on the line, please meet a guy called Art,
He wants you all to listen and he says, "That's real smart."

You'll know about this Jesus who those Romans crucified,
But he gave his friends instructions just the night before he
    died,
Said, "Wait here in Jerus'lem, there's a gift got to be given;
He's the Spirit of the Living God, an' he's coming down
    from heaven!"

The disciples got
    together and they all began to pray.
One hundred and a-twenty were just
    waiting for that day.
Then suddenly one morning, with a shriek and with a
    wail,

A violent wind from heaven filled the
whole house with a gale!

238

There was fire in the air and the glow began to spread
Until each of the disciples had a flame upon his head.
They all began to laugh and shout, for not a soul was
  burnt,
But each could speak a language that none of them had
  learnt!

Well the people heard the racket and
  thousands came a-running,
But to hear their own language spoke now that was really
  stunning!
Then Peter took the lead and said, "This ain't no drunken
                                  rave,
                      The Son of God was crucified,
                        but he's risen from the grave!

You people are just full of sin, your
  lives need a new start,

Let Jesus sort the mess out, he's got power to change your
    heart."
Three thousand got the message then, three thousand all
    believed,
Three thousand got baptised that day, and new life they
    received.

Now you may have heard some rappin' and some
    laughing and some clapping
Caught the rhyming and the rhythm till your fingers started
    snapping
But until the Holy Spirit comes and sets your heart on fire
There's no power in all the earth that'll ever take you
    higher.
Said, no power in all the earth that'll ever
    take you
    higher.

Thanks to Rev Ian Blake of St Christopher's, Sneinton, Nottingham, for
the original idea

52 Ideas for Junior Classroom Assemblies

by Chris Chesterton and Pat Gutteridge

Assembly outlines, readings, dramas and activities for use in junior schools with individual classes and larger groups.

This book is designed to fit Key Stage Two of the National Curriculum. It is divided into three major sections. Stories from the Old Testament; Stories from the New Testament; and Life's Big Questions. The book is in a large easy-to-photocopy format and the price includes a licence to photocopy. Both authors have extensive experience of leading assemblies and training teachers.

Features include:

- Requires minimum preparation by teacher
- All information needed is supplied in book
- Over 60 pages of material for photocopying (licence included in price)
- Extra strong binding
- Maximum pupil participation
- Themes directly related to children's experience

Monarch
Publications

ISBN 1 85424 291 1
256pp large format
Price £14.99

School Assemblies Need You!

by Richard Dyter

For many of us, schools are a separate world. However, schools are keen to build links with local communities, and many are looking for outside help with their assemblies. Such schools actively welcome trustworthy Christian visitors.

Christian parents, governors and churches have an opportunity as never before to get involved in assemblies. This book addresses basic questions: What do I say? How do I say it? How do I approach schools? How can I get a team together? What are the pitfalls?

Richard Dyter includes ten sample assembly scripts and provides a list of useful contacts and resources. This is a practical, straightforward guide on how Christians can make a real impact in our schools.

Richard Dyter is a freelance writer based in Newcastle-upon-Tyne, where he takes assemblies at a local inner-city school. After studying at Oxford and in Japan, he worked in advertising before starting his writing career.

Co-published with Care for Education

Monarch
Publications

ISBN 1 85424 359 4
224pp large format
Price £7.99

Bullying:
What *Can* Parents Do?

by Kevin Brown

Bullying is a widespread social problem, both in school and at home. Bullying does not just involve a minority of children. It affects all of us in one way or another – and not simply as bullies or victims. Bullying covers a vast range of behaviour, and parents themselves are often caught up in it. Kevin Brown's research has shown that parents and teachers who get involved often do so in ways that make the problem worse. The common forms of intervention used by parents and teachers fall into the categories of rescuing, indifference and punishment, which can perpetuate the bullying cycle.

Kevin Brown presents a comprehensive re-examination of the bullying phenomenon. He argues that we need to grasp what it means to see ourselves as people of worth. In establishing our own value we are less likely to become either victims or bullies. Through an understanding of Jesus' mission we can find a sense of self-worth which we need to pass on to our children. *If your child is a victim, or a bully, this book can help.*

Kevin Brown has substantial experience as a social worker and educationalist. He is now a freelance trainer and author living in Penicuik, Scotland. He has written extensively about bullying in schools, and has produced a novel, videos and classroom material on this subject. He and his wife have five children.

Monarch
Publications

ISBN 1 85424 361 6
160pp large format
Price £7.99